DEACON DAVID LOCHBIHLER, J.D.

JOYFUL SOLITUDE

ORTHODOX LOGOS PUBLISHING

JOYFUL SOLITUDE

by Deacon David Lochbihler, J.D.

Front Cover photograph by Alicia Wiley Photography
Back Cover photograph by Tania Xiong-Lochbihler
About the Author photograph by Harry William Reineke IV

Book cover design and interior layout by Max Mendor

Publishers Maxim Hodak & Max Mendor

© 2023, Deacon David Lochbihler, J.D.

© 2023, Orthodox Logos Publishing,

The Netherlands

www.orthodoxlogos.com

ISBN: 978-1-80484-088-7
ISBN: 978-1-80484-089-4

This book is in copyright. No part of this publication may be reproduced, stored in a retrieval system or transmitted in any form or by any means without the prior permission in writing of the publisher, nor be otherwise circulated in any form of binding or cover other than that in which it is published without a similar condition, including this condition, being imposed on the subsequent purchaser.

DEACON DAVID LOCHBIHLER, J.D.

JOYFUL SOLITUDE

ORTHODOX LOGOS PUBLISHING

CONTENTS

Acknowledgements 11

Prologue – Still Silence in the Sacristy 15

Chapter One – Desiring Silence 22

Chapter Two – Seeking Stillness 34

Chapter Three – Celebrating Solitude 41

Chapter Four – Essential Emptiness 48

Chapter Five – Embracing Loneliness 55

Chapter Six – Still Silence 67

Chapter Seven – Joyful Solitude 75

Epilogue – Still Silence During the Divine Liturgy . . . 84

Bibliography 91

About the Author 99

To Millie Ruth

A Poem for Mass
by
Millie Ruth Frazier

I raise my eyes and turn towards the Altar,
I bow my head and pray!
Glory be to the Father,
and to the Son,
and to the Holy Ghost.
As it was in the beginning,
is now, and ever shall be,
world without end! Amen.
I kneel to take Communion.
I am heavy.
I am weak.
I am dirty and scared.
But when I take Communion
I am clean,
I am light,
I am strong,
and I am full of hope.
I know God is with me!

ACKNOWLEDGEMENTS

A heartfelt thank you to His Grace Bishop John for ordaining me to the Holy Diaconate at Saint Patrick Orthodox Church while celebrating the Feast of Saint Patrick on Sunday 17 March 2019 and His Grace Bishop Thomas for being such a true and faithful friend to our church community for many years. God grant you both many years.

After receiving the Master of Arts degree in Applied Orthodox Theology from Balamand University and the Antiochian House of Studies on Thursday 31 August 2017, I reflected upon my five superb summers at the Antiochian Village in Bolivar, Pennsylvania. The words of both Bishops John and Thomas at the Village and other holy gatherings during the years continue to touch my heart.

Although "many distractions call us away from God, the call to holiness makes us authentic. The world is looking for authenticity."[1] In our everyday lives, Bishop John offered superb advice by challenging us to "become invisible so that Christ in us can be seen."[2] In this regard, we need to "listen more and talk less."[3] In discerning our vocation, "God knows what you need even better than you do. God sees you outside

---

[1] His Grace Bishop John, Western Rite Vicariate Conference, 9 August 2018, St. Peter Orthodox Church, Fort Worth, TX, Lecture.

[2] Ibid.

[3] Ibid.

time. He sees the big picture and knows best where you can serve Him."[4]

Bishop Thomas enjoys talking about our Orthodox churches and schools. The Orthodox Church is "a hospital of sinners to save souls."[5] A former educator, Bishop Thomas understands how important it is that "the children in our schools are trained to remain upright citizens in the kingdom of God."[6] We are blessed at Saint Patrick to be finishing the second year of our new Orthodox school. The children at this superb school are immersed in prayer. As one fourth-grade scholar describing a typical day wrote to me, "First we do Prime or Mass, then we do our Morning Litany, and then we read about our Saint."[7] In a subsequent letter, this Orthodox student wrote, "I love Prime & Mass. My prayer life with Jesus and Mary is magnificent."[8]

I am eternally grateful to Metropolitan Kallistos Ware of blessed memory, Father Peter Gillquist of blessed memory, his beloved wife Khouria Marilyn Gillquist, and Father Alexander Atty of blessed memory for guiding and inspiring me during my wondrous Orthodoxy journey.

My family gathered last summer to celebrate Mom's one hundredth birthday, and there is much joy whenever I visit

....

[4] Ibid.

[5] His Grace Bishop Thomas, Antiochian House of Studies, 3 September 2015, Antiochian Village Conference Center, Bolivar, PA, Graduation Banquet.

[6] His Grace Bishop Thomas, Antiochian House of Studies, 2 September 2015, Antiochian Village Conference Center, Bolivar, PA, Lecture.

[7] Millie Ruth Frazier, Letter to David Lochbihler, 13 September 2022.

[8] Millie Ruth Frazier, Letter to David Lochbihler, 11 September 2022.

with my older siblings Fred, Lyn, and Vince and their families. A special welcome to our family's two latest additions. Frederick Fuechee Lochbihler V is the son of my nephew Frederick Karlman IV and Tania Xiong, the grandson of my brother Frederick Vincent III, Notre Dame Class Valedictorian of 1973, the great-grandson of my beloved father and best friend Frederick Louis II (1910-1983) of blessed memory, and the great-great-grandson of my grandfather Frederick Joseph (1879-1949) of blessed memory. Frederick Fuechee's baby sister Leilala Hli Nra joined the Lochbihler family on Friday 1 July 2022. You may catch Fuechee's smile on the back cover of this publication!

The wonder-filled people of Saint Patrick Orthodox Church are simply the best. Thank you to Father Patrick Cardine, Deacon Douglas King, and all the Sons of Saint Patrick, our superb Subdeacons, magnificent Masters of Ceremony, terrific Thurifers, amazing Acolytes, and brilliant Boat Bearers. The camaraderie within our Sacristy nurtures a holy bond of lifelong friendship. Our brilliant choir led by gifted music directors Khouria Kerrie Cardine and Jacob Lash and our prayerful parishioners in the pews continually bring immense joy to my heart.

Professional and collegial thanks to David and Jo Thoburn, Dean of Students Anthony Pangle, Dean of Operations Angela Etter, Dean of Academics Isabel Craun, fourth-grade colleague Kimberly Dow, Cardinal Chess colleague Benjamin Garber, and our exceptional scholars at The Fairfax Christian School in Dulles, Virginia, the finest school in the Commonwealth of Virginia. Let me share a most joyful fourth-grade classroom experience from earlier this year. Mom recently called me at school while I taught my fourth-grade students. We are not supposed to take personal calls at school, but even in the middle of a lecture, when you see there is a very rare telephone call during work hours from your one-hundred-year-old mother, you pick up.

With Mom on the telephone in front of one of my classes for the first time in my three-decade career, a great idea popped into my head. "Hey, everybody, let's all sing Happy Birthday to my mom. She just turned one hundred this summer!"

My fourth graders sang loudly and magnificently.

A special thank you to my fourth-grade scholars at The Fairfax Christian School in Dulles, Virginia: the Class of 2029 for their joyful enthusiasm, the Class of 2030 for inspiring me to excel, and the Class of 2031 for encouraging me to write.

This work would not be worthy of print without the expert editing advice of my friend Scott Richardson. After a thorough substantive and theological analysis of my manuscripts, Scott goes the extra mile to discover with painstaking patience the most minute of typographical errors. Finally, a profound, professional thank you to Maxim Hodak and Max Mendor of Stichting Orthodox Logos and Ksenia Papazova, the Managing Editor of Glagoslav Publications, in Nederland, for publishing this my fourth book. Your deep love for our true and timeless Orthodox faith inspires.

Friends in Jesus & Mary, Saints & Angels,
Deacon David Lochbihler
Saint Patrick Orthodox Church
Tuesday 13 December 2022
Feast of Saint Lucy
orthodoxdeacondavid@gmail.com

PROLOGUE:

STILL SILENCE IN THE SACRISTY

"Assuredly, I say to you, whatever you bind on earth will be bound in heaven, and whatever you loose on earth will be loosed in heaven. Again I say to you that if two of you agree on earth concerning anything that they ask, it will be done for them by My Father in heaven. For where two or three are gathered together in My name, I am there in the midst of them" (Matthew 18:19-20 NKJV).

A global pandemic rocked our world.

I was blessed. Mom at the age of one hundred has been vaccinated and playing cards with her friends in Wauwatosa, Wisconsin. My church with courage and grace worshipped together, added converts, and nurtured friendships. My school, mandated by the State to do daily temperature checks, wear masks, and social distance, captured a Virginia state basketball championship. After the online learning during the initial spring statewide stay-at-home orders, our school returned in the fall and did not miss a single day in the classroom, and despite rigid governmental restrictions, not one of my fantastic fourth graders whined or complained.

Yet not everyone was so blessed. One lifelong friend from New York, a city stunned by the ferocity of this dreaded disease in the very early days of the pandemic, lost dozens of family members and close friends. Some of our friends lost someone. Still others contracted the disease, suffered, and recovered. Too many of our friends lost their jobs and their livelihoods, facing financial ruin. Nations around the world, from Great Britain to Germany, from Italy to India, from Egypt to Ethiopia, from Brazil to Bangladesh, were brought to their knees by tragic tears and our great mutual enemy, death.

I was blessed beyond measure to worship freely and not miss a single day of work at school while still receiving several stimulus checks. Others were not so lucky, battling this disease, losing their jobs, or attending school online for an entire school year. Many of us spent more time at home than usual, masked at the local grocery store, and faced the ultimate decision in battling adversity in life: Given these circumstances, do I choose to become bitter or better?

Which leads to the choice ultimately facing all of us, either during a global pandemic or upon facing disease and our inevitable deathbed: Do I choose joy or despair? We all are dying, and death is the ultimate solitude. Call it what you will, but upon facing death, even if we are surrounded by loving family and lifelong friends, we die alone.

Or do we?

Prior to our Pentecost Vigil morning service, with the baptismal font and Mass preparations readied, I sat in the Sacristy at Saint Patrick Orthodox Church in Virginia with Subdeacon John Wiley and Acolyte Kai. We discussed the essence and depth of silence and solitude.

"Now in the morning, having risen a long while before daylight, He went out and departed to a solitary place; and there He prayed."[9] Jesus grew up with a wonderful family and

---

[9] Mark 1:35 NKJV.

was intimately immersed in His faith. Despite being engaged in a busy and active ministry, Jesus experienced a profound and ongoing union and communion with His Heavenly Father. Why do our busy lives make it so difficult to better fulfil this inner yearning for prayer? During our Sacristy conversation, Subdeacon John Wiley eloquently said, "Our whole lives today are structured to distract us from personal reflection."[10] From our ever-ringing iPhones, the interesting ideas on our iPads, and the wide reach of social media, television, and movies, it is not surprising we are distracted and find it difficult to pray. Jesus prayed in still silence and encountered God. In our hectic and hurried lives, is it any surprise that we cannot?

Perhaps you strive to seek God with a quiet walk in the woods. The poet Gerard Manley Hopkins beheld the beauty of nature and declared, "The world is charged with the grandeur of God."[11] Even when we walk in wonder, however, our minds beholding God's grandeur still face the incessant interruption of our typical tyrannical thoughts. This walk in the woods though special is not still silence.

You may decide to read a superb Orthodox theological book written by one of the giants of our faith like Father Joseph Allen, Father Peter Gillquist, Father Vladimir Lossky, and Father Alexander Schmemann, four superb Orthodox authors, all of blessed memory, penning multiple manuscripts well-read by so many of us and sitting on our bookshelves. Subdeacon John Wiley made an excellent point during our Sacristy pre-liturgical discussion: Even while doing such a

---

[10] Subdeacon John Wiley Gebhardt, personal communication, Saint Patrick Orthodox Church, Bealeton, VA, 19 June 2021.

[11] Gerard Manley Hopkins, *Poems of Gerard Manley Hopkins*, ed. W. H. Gardner (New York: Oxford University Press, 1948), 70.

great thing like reading, our minds although eternally enriched are far from silent; they are active and engaged. Reading is good yet not still silence.

There must be another way to encounter God. Surely all of us worshiping within the Orthodox Church, the truest and dearest community of faith, can discover the silence and stillness of deep and abiding prayer in our lives.

Perhaps you pray *Lectio Divina* or the Divine Office in the Monastic Diurnal. You speak slowly, you try to concentrate. Yet your mind still may wander. Your Diurnal ribbons may be on the wrong page and need to be moved. You read the Psalms yet if asked immediately afterwards, you have no recollection of what you just read. Father Edward Hughes challenged us during a Lenten Retreat several years ago to pray our next Divine Office as if it were our last. I fail to do this. God loves our effort, we try to do our best, yet this is not still silence.

You may love to sit in your favourite chair at home or on the porch and simply try to pray to God with no distractions. There is very little noise, and you find yourself surrounded by a nearly complete silence. Yet often in this prayerful stance, my mind still races, filled with an overabundance of random thoughts. I try to pray, yet is my prayer directed to God, or am I talking only to myself? This attempt at prayer though valiant is not still silence.

Perhaps this is what we seek, this is what we want deep down inside: "Be still, and know that I am God."[12] We need to slow down. We need to stop. We need to rest. We need to empty our minds moving a million miles a minute. To begin our earnest and eternal quest towards God, our Triune Trin-

....

[12] Psalm 46:10a KJV.

ity shrouded in indescribable mystery – Our Heavenly Father omnipresent yet hidden, our Crucified and Risen Christ fully divine and fully human, our Holy Ghost the Pure Paraclete – we need to first simply seek to be still. After stillness follows silence:

> My soul, wait in silence for God only,
> For my hope is from Him.[13]

For me, the key word within this verse is "wait." Not just try to be silent, but to "wait in silence." For truly, "my hope is from Him," and prayer is not about us, but all about Him. Striving for stillness, waiting in silence, is a good first step. "But you, when you pray, go into your room, and when you have shut your door, pray to your Father who *is* in the secret *place*; and your Father who sees in secret will reward you openly."[14]

Author Kyriacos Markides in *The Mountain of Silence* travels with Father Maximos, a Mount Athos monk, around Cyprus, the island in the eastern Mediterranean Sea. He learned there is a great difference between loneliness and being alone. Father Maximos expressed this difference in describing a meeting with a man living in almost completely isolation. "I remember years ago I met a hermit on Mount Athos who lived by himself in the wilderness. I asked him, 'Father, aren't you afraid to live here all alone?' His reply was that he could never feel alone since he continuously prayed. He was filled with the living presence of God's love."[15]

---

[13] Psalm 62:5 NASB.

[14] Matthew 6:6 NKJV.

[15] Kyriacos C. Markides, *The Mountain of Silence* (New York: Doubleday, 2001), 202-203.

Subdeacon John Wiley expressed it well. "The key to finding joyful solitude is silence before God."[16] In still silence, we stop talking and start listening. When our minds race, we try to remember the Body and Blood of Christ. When distractions assail us, we try instead to focus on the Name of Jesus or the Love of Our Lady. God is infinite, we are finite, and we can never arrive fully. Yet by trying our best each day, with sincere hearts, our ever-present Triune God is there and meets us wherever and whenever we will to worship in still silence:

> And he said, Go forth, and stand upon the mount before the LORD. And, behold, the LORD passed by, and a great and strong wind rent the mountains, and brake in pieces the rocks before the LORD; *but* the LORD *was* not in the earthquake: And after the earthquake a fire; *but* the LORD *was* not in the fire: and after the fire a still small voice.[17]

Becoming Orthodox opens one's world to wonder like never before. "And now here is my secret, a very simple secret: It is only with the heart that one can see rightly; what is essential is invisible to the eye."[18] With these words, Antoine de Saint-Exupéry describes the essence of seeing our world through the inner eyes of faith. This ongoing quest for the essential and the invisible aptly expresses our lifelong journey towards still silence. God is always there, patiently waiting. Baptized in the Blessed Water, anointed with the Chrism Oil, receiving the Body and Blood of Christ during the Divine

---

[16] Subdeacon John Wiley Gebhardt, 19 June 2021.

[17] 1 Kings 19:11-12 KJV.

[18] Antoine de Saint-Exupéry, *The Little Prince* (San Diego: Harcourt Brace, 1971), 73.

Liturgy, we will in time face suffering, pain, and death, yet because of our Orthodox faith, God is with us, and we are never alone.

"Truly I say to you, unless you are converted and become like children, you shall not enter the kingdom of heaven."[19] To be a child of God means to see again with the inner eyes of faith, to truly wonder. A child is devoted to his or her best friends Jesus and Mary with a pure heart while experiencing joyful humility. Wrapping up our Sacristy sacred session, I asked twelve-year-old Acolyte Kai what he thought, and he responded with superb simplicity, "I like this conversation."[20]

---

[19] Matthew 18:3 NASB.

[20] Kai Friedrich, personal communication, Saint Patrick Orthodox Church, Bealeton, VA, 19 June 2021.

CHAPTER ONE

DESIRING SILENCE

> Set a guard, O Lord, over my mouth;
> Keep watch over the door of my lips.
> Do not incline my heart to any evil thing,
> To practice wicked works
> With men who work iniquity;
> And do not let me eat of their delicacies.
> Let the righteous strike me;
> *It shall be* a kindness.
> And let him rebuke me;
> *It shall be* as excellent oil;
> Let my head not refuse it
> (Psalm 141:3-5 NKJV).

Our spiritual quest begins with the desire for silence. Daily life is far more hectic and distracted than ever before in human history. Compare your drives to the grocery store today with the same shopping trips from decades ago. How many of us today pause after placing eggs and milk in the cart to answer our cell phones or smartphones? We push the cart while talking with someone, the people we pass in the aisles overhearing half of our conversation.

Multitasking is the new normal. Like many things in our world, multitasking, completing two or more tasks simultaneously, offers strengths and weaknesses. On a positive note, people able to balance and expedite several assignments successfully expands work quality and productivity. A fun example of multitasking happens regularly in my fourth-grade classroom. After preparing her loose-leaf paper for the Spelling Test, a scholar will ask for permission to multitask by simultaneously working on an Arithmetic assignment. As I read the Spelling word and a sentence, the fourth grader will both write the word and begin an Arithmetic problem before the next Spelling word is read. Learning to perform under pressure, from the classroom to the basketball court, is an important life skill in the 21st century.

Yet multitasking offers an array of challenging negatives. If work is not done carefully, avoidable mistakes may be made. The most successful fourth-grade spellers share two traits in common. First, they study; second, they check their work. By hurrying through two assignments in Spelling and Arithmetic simultaneously, silly mistakes may be made in both tasks preventable by a little more careful focus upon each. The mission remains to finish the assignment with excellence rather than merely completing the chore. Even the busyness of business requires some thoughtful silence.

Silence is where we must begin our journey. We need to take a step back from our exceptionally busy lives in three simple ways: walk, prayer, and worship.

I love walks at the Warrenton Branch Greenway near the downtown area of my small town in Virginia. This old railroad, built in the middle of the 19th century, has been converted into a superb walking and biking trail extending more than two miles each way, the pathway located right next to where I live. An old-fashioned walk surrounded by the swaying leaves of trees is a wonderful small step towards silence.

The poet William Wordsworth understood the relevance of silence by inviting scholars to pause from their books in order to "Let Nature be your teacher."[21]

Although finite creatures, we catch a partial glimpse of our infinite God through His creation:

> The heavens declare the glory of God;
> And the firmament shows His handiwork.
> Day unto day utters speech,
> And night unto night reveals knowledge.[22]

When we walk in nature, God extends a gentle invitation to surround our hearts in silence and meet Him through His most wonder-full creation. We need to desire this silence. Walking to think through problems and resolve issues is not desiring silence. Walking while listening to a prayerful CD is not desiring silence. Regular walks on the Warrenton Branch Greenway for me usually involve reading the Monastic Diurnal, reciting the Rosary, or lifting the names of people I know, family and friends, living and deceased, in my daily prayer. Although good activities in and of themselves, these summer prayer walks occupy my mind rather than nurture a desire for silence within my heart.

Perhaps a different approach is to begin desiring silence at home while tying your shoes just before leaving the house. Then try simply to go for a walk surrounded by trees with no gameplan, no agenda, and no noise. Just walk and listen. Let creation give you a limited glimpse of the Creator:

---

[21] William Wordsworth, "The Tables Turned," *Selected Poems of William Wordsworth*, ed. Solomon Francis Gingerich (Boston: Houghton Mifflin Company, 1923), 7.

[22] Psalm 139:1-2 NKJV.

> And I have felt
> A presence that disturbs me with the joy
> Of elevated thoughts; a sense sublime
> Of something far more deeply interfused,
> Whose dwelling is the light of setting suns,
> And the round ocean and the living air,
> And the blue sky, and in the mind of man;
> A motion and a spirit, that impels
> All thinking things, all objects of all thought,
> And rolls through all things. Therefore am I still
> A lover of the meadows and the woods,
> And mountains; and of all that we behold
> From this green earth; of all the mighty world
> Of eye, and ear, – both what they half create,
> And what perceive; well pleased to recognise
> In nature and the language of the sense,
> The anchor of my purest thoughts, the nurse,
> The guide, the guardian of my heart, and soul
> Of all my moral being.[23]

Simply desire silence. "And for all this, nature is never spent; There lives the dearest freshness deep down things."[24]

Walking in nature amidst the tall trees and beautiful birds is one way to seek silence. Yet God invites us to a deeper encounter. "Cross with your mind from the visible things to the invisible, from the created world to the Creator."[25] A second

---

[23] William Wordsworth, "Lines 93b-111," *Selected Poems of William Wordsworth*, ed. Solomon Francis Gingerich, 11-12.

[24] Gerard Manley Hopkins, "God's Grandeur," *Poems of Gerard Manley Hopkins*, 70.

[25] Saint Tikhon of Voronezh, *On True Christianity*, vol.1, translated by Marianna Lilley (Waynesboro, VA: Old Paths Press, 2020), 37.

opportunity to embrace silence occurs whenever we try to pray.

Prayer takes innumerable forms. To be honest, I have to admit much if not most of my time in life spent praying was not even prayer at all. Too numerous to count are the instances when my mind wandered during Mass, I sped through the Divine Office, or personal prayer begun in earnest devolves into revolving thoughts in my mind where I talk to myself rather than try to talk and listen to God. Despite our meager offerings, our infinite heavenly Father patiently waits to welcome us into union and communion with Him every minute of every day, and all we need to do is ask.

Prior to personal prayer, we need to sit silently and ponder the power and presence of sin in our lives. "You see a man clothed in rags, half-naked, and disfigured with deformities. Turn your mind from this to the sinful soul, which is stripped naked of the grace of God as of beautiful clothing, and is instead covered in sinful deformities as in rags. A disfigured man is repulsive before human eyes, but the soul disfigured by sinful filth is even more repulsive before the eyes of God. This occasion exhorts you to avoid every sin, which disfigures the soul and makes it unworthy of the sight of God."[26]

As a child attending Roman Catholic grade and high schools, the image of a white, pure soul was learned early and remains embedded deeply in my heart and memory. Sins would add black spots to the holy, unspotted soul, only removed with a sincere and heartfelt Confession. I vividly remember walking down the side and up the middle aisle at Saint Charles Borromeo Church in grade school after Con-

---

[26] Saint Tikhon of Voronezh, *From Things Earthly to Things Heavenly*, translated by Marianna Lilley (Waynesboro, VA: Old Paths Press, 2020), 28.

fession, my heart overflowing with a pure and abundant joy. The joyful power of the Sacrament of Confession enhances our experience of the Real Presence of Christ in Holy Communion.

Our childlike memories embolden our adult journeys of faith. In battling sin in our lives, we need to delve deeply into our hearts and reject anything and everything separating us from God. "The Gospel teaches us to cut off the roots of our sins and not merely their fruits."[27] This requires the silence of a listening heart:

> I said, I will take heed to my ways, that I sin not with my tongue: I will keep my mouth with a bridle, while the wicked is before me. I was dumb with silence, I held my peace, even from good; and my sorrow was stirred. My heart was hot within me, while I was musing the fire burned: then spake I with my tongue, LORD, make me to know mine end, and the measure of my days, what it is: that I may know how frail I am.[28]

To make real and intimate prayer possible, our hearts must be pure, our lives must be holy: "Therefore gird up the loins of your mind, be sober, and rest *your* hope fully upon the grace that is to be brought to you at the revelation of Jesus Christ; as obedient children, not conforming yourselves to the former lusts, *as* in your ignorance; but as He who called you *is* holy, you also be holy in all *your* conduct, because it is

---

[27] Saint John Cassian, "On the Eight Vices," *The Philokalia*, vol. 1, compiled by Saint Nikodemos and Saint Makarios, translated and edited by G.E.H. Palmer, Philip Sherrard, and Kallistos Ware (New York: Faber and Faber, 1979), 86.

[28] Psalm 39:1-4 KJV.

written, '*Be holy, for I am holy.*'"[29] This holiness begins with an honest Confession and is constantly confirmed with frequent Holy Communion.

Once forgiven of sin, we are free to love and live for God. "Rejoice evermore. Pray without ceasing. In every thing give thanks: for this is the will of God in Christ Jesus concerning you."[30] Our heart's response described by Saint Paul becomes a daily reality: we rejoice not occasionally but always; we pray not just on Sunday but without ceasing; our hearts overflow with gratitude. We worship the Holy Trinity and venerate the Holy Mother, praying to both with joyful and loving hearts.

Although prayer begins with a desire for silence, this silence must not become an end in itself. The silence is not the end, but the means to the end, and the end is God. "The goal, the experience we must seek, is communion with the divine."[31] We can quiet the heart and sit silently yet draw no closer to God, proud of our ability to achieve a sense of peaceful calm. Deep personal prayer begins with silence while actively seeking God. Our mission is simple: "Casting down imaginations, and every high thing that exalteth itself against the knowledge of God, and bringing into captivity every thought to the obedience of Christ."[32] For Roman Catholic Trappist monk Thomas Merton, citing the Desert Fathers and the *Philokalia*, "prayer of the heart (is) a way of keeping oneself in the presence of God and of reality, rooted in one's

---

[29] 1 Peter 1:13-16 NKJV.

[30] 1 Thessalonians 5:16-18 KJV.

[31] Metropolitan Philip Saliba and Joseph J. Allen, *Meeting the Incarnate God* (Brookline, MA: Holy Cross Orthodox Press, 2009), 9.

[32] 2 Corinthians 10:5 KJV.

own inner truth."[33] We try to meet God where we are at, yet our prayer purpose must strive to seek God rather than merely talk to ourselves.

How do we cast down our imaginations and take every thought captive for Christ? The best course to proceed in personal prayer is Sacred Scriptures, as God speaks directly to our hearts through His Holy Word. We begin by recognizing our connection to Christ: "I am the vine, ye *are* the branches: He that abideth in me, and I in him, the same bringeth forth much fruit: for without me ye can do nothing."[34] His Eminence Metropolitan Kallistos Ware of blessed memory described a most powerful and effective "type of personal prayer which has for many centuries played an extraordinarily important part in the life of Orthodoxy – the Jesus Prayer: "*Lord Jesus Christ, Son of God, have mercy on me.*"[35]

I attended a lecture by Metropolitan Kallistos at Saint Mark Coptic Church in Fairfax, Virginia, in 2012. He eloquently elaborated upon a variety of ways to pray the Jesus Prayer. First, the Jesus Prayer may include the entire community, even the entire world: "Lord Jesus Christ, Son of God, have mercy on us." Second, the Jesus Prayer may be penitential: "Lord Jesus Christ, Son of God, have mercy on me, the sinner." Third, the Jesus Prayer may be shorter: "Lord Jesus, have mercy." Fourth, the Jesus Prayer may be made through the Blessed Virgin Mary: "Lord Jesus Christ, at the prayers of the Mother of God, have mercy on me." Finally, the Jesus Prayer may be made through the Saints: "Lord Jesus Christ, at the prayers of Saint Patrick,

---

[33] Thomas Merton, *Contemplative Prayer* (Garden City, NY: Image Books, 1971), 23.

[34] John 15:5 KJV.

[35] Timothy Ware, *The Orthodox Church* (London: Penguin Books, 1997), 304 (emphasis in original).

have mercy on me."³⁶ During the nearly one decade since attending this lecture, I have added a few prayers of my own:

Abba Father, Lord Jesus;
Holy Ghost, Virgin Mary

Pure Patros, Logos Love;
Sanctus Spiritus, Trinity Truth

Boy Jesus, Crucified Christ;
Virgin Mary, Theotokos

Corpus Christi, Precious Blood;
Eat My Flesh, Drink My Blood

(The names of two or three Saints);
Trinity, Theotokos

"Metropolitan Kallistos spoke about how to incorporate the Jesus Prayer into our daily lives. As described so eloquently by Metropolitan Kallistos during his talk, like Moses at the Burning Bush, we Orthodox stand on holy ground, and our faith is immersed in awe and wonder. God created us to pray, and without prayer in our lives we are not fully human. During our prayerful silence, we listen intently for the presence of God. From the stillness of prayer, Jesus offered words of fire and healing, acts of power and transformation. Like Jesus, from the silence and stillness of our prayer, we embrace

....

[36] Metropolitan Kallistos Ware, "The Jesus Prayer in our Daily Lives," Saint Mark Coptic Orthodox Church, 23 June 2012, Fairfax, VA, Lecture.

others with words of healing, with acts of love."[37] As stated by Metropolitan Kallistos, "Prayer is a personal dialogue: the Holy Trinity and I."[38]

Our silence in prayer is imbued with eternal depth and definition to the extent we fill it with the name of Jesus while our hearts expand to seek the Holy Trinity. "To pronounce the name of Jesus in a holy way is an all-sufficient and surpassing aim for any human life."[39] The silence we desire in prayer leaves room for the name of Jesus and in time a personal dialogue with the Holy Trinity. "The revelation of God the Holy Trinity–Father, Son and Holy Spirit is the basis of all Christian theology; it is, indeed, theology itself, in the sense in which that word was understood by the Greek Fathers, for whom *theology* most commonly stood for the mystery of the Trinity revealed to the Church."[40]

Besides walking in the woods and personal prayer, we desire silence through our worship during the Divine Liturgy. "In the Orthodox Church, each Sunday is the day of resurrection and each Eucharist a Pentecost."[41] Serving at the Holy Altar as a Deacon at Saint Patrick Orthodox Church in Virginia brings indescribable joy to my heart during every Divine Liturgy in which I am blessed and privileged to serve.

---

[37] Deacon David Lochbihler, *The Joy of Orthodoxy* (Nederland: Orthodox Logos, 2022), 108.

[38] Metropolitan Kallistos Ware, "The Jesus Prayer in our Daily Lives," Saint Mark Coptic Orthodox Church, 23 June 2012.

[39] Archimandrite Lev Gillet, *The Jesus Prayer* (Crestwood, NY: St. Vladimir's Seminary Press, 1987), 41.

[40] Vladimir Lossky, *The Mystical Theology of the Eastern Church* (Crestwood, NY: St. Vladimir's Seminary Press, 1976), 67 (emphasis in original).

[41] Alexander Schmemann, *For the Life of the World*, 2nd ed. (Crestwood, NY: St. Vladimir's Seminary Press, 1973), 55.

We truly stand on holy ground: "The church is the temple of God, a holy place, a house of prayer, the assembly of the people, the body of Christ. It is called the bride of Christ. It is cleansed by the water of His baptism, sprinkled by His blood, clothed in bridal garments, and sealed with the ointment of the Holy Spirit."[42] Our Western Rite parish celebrates Lauds and Mass each Sunday morning using the ancient Gregorian Chant. Our services are timeless. Nearly every single Sunday, the more than two hours of prayer and worship seem no longer than fifteen or twenty minutes. Time seems not to exist as God "raised *us* up together, and made *us* sit together in the heavenly *places* in Christ Jesus."[43]

"The church is an earthly heaven in which the supercelestial God dwells and walks about."[44] Near the turn of the first millennium,

> Vladimir, Prince of Kiev, while still a pagan, desired to know which was the true religion, and therefore sent his followers to visit the various countries of the world in turn. ... the Muslim Bulgars of the Volga ... Germany and Rome ... Finally they journeyed to Constantinople, and here at last, as they attended to the Divine Liturgy in the great Church of the Holy Wisdom, they discovered what they desired. "We knew not whether we were in heaven or on earth, for surely there is no such splendour or beauty anywhere upon earth. We cannot describe it to you: only this we know, that *God dwells there among*

---

[42] Saint Germanus of Constantinople, *On the Divine Liturgy*, translated by Paul Meyendorff (Crestwood, NY: St. Vladimir's Seminary Press, 1984), 57.

[43] Ephesians 2:6 NKJV.

[44] Saint Germanus of Constantinople, *On the Divine Liturgy*, 57.

> *humans*, and that their service surpasses the worship of all other places. For we cannot forget that beauty."[45]

The Divine Liturgy is a source of indescribable joy. "Heaven on earth,"[46] this is exactly how I feel during Mass each Sunday at Saint Patrick Orthodox Church, especially while assisting our Priest at the Holy Altar. I see the Holy Icons, understand the Real Presence of the Corpus Christi in the Tabernacle each time I genuflect, and believe an array of Angels and Saints attend our worship.

Two moments during the Mass touch my heart in a most memorable way: the consecration of the bread and wine into the Body and Blood of Christ and the reception of Holy Communion. These are two liturgical times of intense focus, two miraculous moments we miss if our hearts are not still and silently worshipping in awe and wonder. A third timeless moment occurs whenever I am blessed by being called upon the chant the Holy Gospel. "St. Jerome († 420) speaks of the deacon as reader of the Gospel."[47] Within the Orthodox Church, East and West, we experience the miracle of heaven on earth every time we celebrate the Divine Liturgy. This experience requires a humble and heartfelt silence.

Walking in the woods, personal prayer at home, worshipping the Holy Trinity during the Divine Liturgy at our Orthodox Churches: with silent hearts, truly being present and listening, we may catch a glimpse of the divine.

---

[45] Timothy Ware, *The Orthodox Church*, 264 (emphasis added).

[46] Alexander Schmemann, *For the Life of the World*, 30.

[47] Adrian Fortescue, *The Mass: A Study of the Roman Liturgy*, 2nd ed. (London: Longmans, Green and Co., 1937), 280.

CHAPTER TWO

SEEKING STILLNESS

> Blessed *is the man* You choose,
> And cause to approach *You*,
> *That* he may dwell in Your courts.
> We shall be satisfied with the goodness of Your house,
> Of Your holy temple.
> *By* awesome deeds in righteousness You will answer us,
> O God of our salvation,
> *You who are* the confidence of all the ends of the earth,
> And of the far-off seas;
> Who established the mountains by His strength,
> *Being* clothed with power;
> You who still the noise of the seas,
> The noise of their waves,
> And the tumult of the peoples
> (Psalm 65:4-7 NKJV).

It brought great joy to my heart to discover the day of my Chrismation fell on one of my favourite feasts of the church calendar: Sunday 8 September 2013, the Feast of the Nativity of the Blessed Virgin Mary. Just as the Incarnation and Birth of Jesus irrevocably changed the world, so too in a mysterious way, the Birth of Mary the Theotokos set the stage for the most remarkable half-century of human history. This special feast marks a memorable beginning.

Love and devotion to Our Lady deepens our communion with Jesus Christ. "Both the virginity of Mary and her giving birth escaped the notice of the prince of this age, as did the Lord's death–three mysteries of a cry, wrought in the stillness of God."[48] The angel Gabriel appeared to Mary during the Annunciation. "How did the highly favoured Virgin, with her unrivalled and holy understanding, respond to these words? She ran to God and reached out to Him in prayer."[49] We must always remember Mary did not have to say yes; she was free to say no. "And Mary said, Behold the handmaid of the Lord; be it unto me according to thy word."[50] The assent of the Holy Virgin and the presence of the Holy Child within her womb transformed our world like never before. "And the angel departed from her, leaving the Maker of all united with a body within her womb. By means of this union, which was the object of his ministry, he had procured salvation for the world."[51]

The Blessed Virgin Mary undoubtedly sought the silence of stillness as her constant companion and friend. "Be still and know that I *am* God."[52] Amidst an array of activities during

---

[48] Saint Ignatius of Antioch, "The Letters of Ignatius of Antioch: Ephesians 19:1," translated by Robert M. Grant, *The Order of St. Ignatius of Antioch*, 5th ed. (Englewood, NJ: Order of St. Ignatius of Antioch, 2006), 82.

[49] Saint Gregory Palamas, *Mary the Mother of God: Sermons by Saint Gregory Palamas,* edited by Christopher Veniamin (South Canaan, PA: Mount Thabor Publishing, 2005), 58.

[50] Luke 1:38a KJV.

[51] Saint Gregory Palamas, *Mary the Mother of God: Sermons by Saint Gregory Palamas,* 58.

[52] Psalm 46:10a NKJV.

the day, Mary would need to seek God, and He is best found in stillness. God is the ultimate Mystery, and to contemplate this Mystery, Mary learned to be still. "The Greek noun *mysterion* is linked with the verb *myein*, meaning 'to close the eyes or mouth.'"[53] When we are not talking and stand in silence, we are free to listen. When we stand in silence and close our eyes, we are free to listen to God.

"Meditate within your heart on your bed, and be still."[54] How much time did the Blessed Virgin Mary devote to prayer each day? "Rejoice always; pray without ceasing; in everything give thanks; for this is God's will for you in Christ Jesus."[55] Joy, Prayer, Thanksgiving: these three virtues must have permeated the heart of the Blessed Virgin Mary throughout her holy childhood.

Joachim and Anna brought Mary to live in the Temple of Jerusalem at the age of three. The three-year-old Mary both received and brought the grace of God. God poured grace upon the child inside the Temple: "There the priest welcomed Mary and kissed her, and blessed her, saying, 'The Lord has magnified your name to all generations of the earth. By you, unto the last of days, the Lord God will reveal redemption to the children of Israel.' Then he sat her down on the third step of the altar, and the Lord God poured out grace upon her. And she danced with her feet, and all the house of Israel loved her."[56] The child brought grace into the temple: "She Herself ascended the high steps and, by revelation from

---

[53] Bishop Kallistos Ware, *The Orthodox Way* (Crestwood, NY: St. Vladimir's Seminary Press, 1995), 15.

[54] Psalm 4:4b NKJV.

[55] 1 Thessalonians 5:16-18 NASB.

[56] Frederica Mathewes-Green, *The Lost Gospel of Mary: The Mother of Jesus in Three Ancient Texts* (Brewster, MA: Paraclete Press, 2007), 43.

God, She was led into the very Holy of Holies, by the High Priest who met Her, taking with Her the grace of God which rested upon Her into the Temple, which until then had been without grace. (See the Kontakion of the Entry into the Temple. This was the newly built Temple into which the glory of God had not descended as it had upon the Ark or upon the Temple of Solomon.)"[57]

Living in the Jerusalem Temple must have been a source of everlasting joy, fervent prayer, and heartfelt thanksgiving. "Mary lived like a nurtured dove in the temple, and received food from the hand of an angel."[58] The twelve-year-old Mary lived and worshipped in the Temple. "Being adorned with all virtues, She manifested an example of extraordinarily pure life."[59] Within a few decades, after a frantic search, Mary would return to the Temple and with great relief find her twelve-year-old Son surrounded by the teachers of the Law.

> The Child continued to grow and become strong, increasing in wisdom; and the grace of God was upon Him. Now His parents went to Jerusalem every year at the Feast of the Passover. And when He became twelve, they went up there according to the custom of the Feast; and as they were returning, after spending the full number of days, the boy Jesus stayed behind in Jerusalem.

---

[57] Saint John Maximovitch, *The Orthodox Veneration of the Mother of God*, translated by Father Seraphim Rose (Platina, CA: St. Herman of Alaska Brotherhood, 2012), 64.

[58] Frederica Mathewes-Green, *The Lost Gospel of Mary: The Mother of Jesus in Three Ancient Texts*, 45.

[59] Saint John Maximovitch, *The Orthodox Veneration of the Mother of God*, 64.

But His parents were unaware of it, but supposed Him to be in the caravan, and went a day's journey; and they began looking for Him among their relatives and acquaintances. When they did not find Him, they returned to Jerusalem looking for Him. Then, after three days they found Him in the temple, sitting in the midst of the teachers, both listening to them and asking them questions. And all who heard Him were amazed at His understanding and His answers. When they saw Him, they were astonished; and His mother said to Him, "Son, why have You treated us this way? Behold, Your father and I have been anxiously looking for You." And He said to them, "Why is it that you were looking for Me? Did you not know that I had to be in My Father's house?" But they did not understand the statement which He had made to them. And He went down with them and came to Nazareth, and He continued in subjection to them; and His mother treasured all these things in her heart. And Jesus kept increasing in wisdom and stature, and in favor with God and men.[60]

"At some point in time, the stark reality of Jesus' absence startled and scared Mary and Joseph to the depth of their being. The caravan traveled from dusk to dawn and pitched their tents one day's journey from Jerusalem."[61] Mary's suffering must have been immense. She must have feared for the safety of her lost Son. "Whenever I am afraid, I will trust in you."[62] Jesus was not lost, yet His Mother did not yet know this.

---

[60] Luke 2:40-52 NASB.

[61] Deacon David Lochbihler (in press), *The Holy Family* [unpublished manuscript].

[62] Psalm 56:3 NKJV.

"This unfortunate circumstance undoubtedly engendered deep anxiety and consternation in the hearts of Mary and Joseph, with the possibility of an emerging despair developing."[63] Mary prayed as a young Mother, perhaps with more intense anguish than ever before. "I sought the Lord and He answered me, And rescued me from all my fears."[64] During her frenzied search for her Child, Mary undoubtedly prayed continually, possibly unceasingly. Perhaps at this time, in the depth of despair, the Theotokos recalled the words of the Archngel Gabriel she had treasured all these years in her heart. "And the angel said unto her, Fear not, Mary: for thou hast found favour with God."[65]

At this time in history, there had not been a finer or more nobler woman alive than the Blessed Virgin Mary. The Child Mary was the greatest human being ever to walk on the face of the earth, prior to the birth of Jesus, prior to Mary becoming the Theotokos, the God-bearer, the Mother of God. "If God the Father chose Her, God the Holy Spirit descended upon Her, and God the Son dwelt in Her, submitted to Her in the days of His youth, was concerned for Her when hanging on the Cross–then should not everyone who confesses the Holy Trinity venerate Her?"[66]

We need to imitate the Blessed Virgin Mary and imitate her by seeking stillness. "Try to make your intellect deaf and dumb during prayer; you will then be able to pray."[67] The

---

[63] Deacon David Lochbihler, *The Holy Family*.

[64] Psalm 34:4 NASB.

[65] Luke 1:30 KJV.

[66] Saint John Maximovitch, *The Orthodox Veneration of the Mother of God*, 21.

[67] Evagrios the Solitary, "On Prayer: One Hundred and Fifty-Three Texts," *The Philokalia*, vol. 1, compiled by Saint Nikodemos and Saint

divine mysteries are simply indescribable and cannot be grasped by the human soul. "But Mary kept all these things and pondered *them* in her heart."[68] We must strive to do the same within the deep stillness of our own hearts.

Makarios, translated and edited by G.E.H. Palmer, Philip Sherrard, and Kallistos Ware (New York: Faber and Faber, 1979), 58.

[68] Luke 2:19 NKJV.

CHAPTER THREE

CELEBRATING SOLITUDE

I have learned in whatever state I am, to be content: I know how to be abased, and I know how to abound. Everywhere and in all things I have learned both to be full and to be hungry, both to abound and to suffer need. I can do all things through Christ who strengthens me (Philippians 4:11b-13 NKJV).

The global pandemic forced all of us to embrace solitude in one form or another.

The Commonwealth of Virginia like most of the world faced a strict lockdown. At my superb private school, we completed the fourth quarter online, joining every single school in our state studying at home during the spring of 2020. Yet that August, we returned to campus for the next academic year and did not miss a single day. I was blessed to teach remarkable fourth-grader scholars, and these two years in the classroom, not missing a beat, were among my finest during nearly three decades as an educator. Despite our daily temperature checks, state mask mandates, social distancing, and a lot of hand sanitizer, my students stayed upbeat, optimistic, and eager to learn.

Best of all, not a single fourth grader whined or complained. There was one close call. We returned after Christmas break in January 2021 with a new government health mandate. For the first two quarters of the school year, a general rule of thumb was "masks while moving," and students with desks far apart in our large classroom were allowed to lower their masks while sitting quietly at their desks. At the beginning of the new year, however, students were required to wear masks even though they were socially distanced while sitting at their desks. I presented this new protocol by combining it with some positive progress being made with vaccines to combat the virus, trying to intersperse both good news and bad news within our new situation.

When told masks had to be worn at all times except while eating or drinking, one fourth grader asked why. Just prior to Christmas we studied the first two chapters of the Gospel of Luke. Recalling two of the angelic encounters with Saint Gabriel, I posed this question to this scholar: "Are you asking 'Why?' like Zechariah or like Mary?" The student pondered and said simply, "Like Mary." He was not whining; he simply sought to understand. With superb scholars like this in our classrooms, we enjoyed another spectacular school year despite the pandemic.

Mom received the vaccine at her independent living community, and now one hundred years old, continues to play cards with her friends. Faced with the inconveniences and burdens of this pandemic, her walk with God has never been stronger. My family was blessed. Yet not everyone was so lucky. One friend shared how more than twenty family and friends were struck during the early months of the disease and suddenly died. Another friend lost someone dear to them. Many people lost their jobs and struggled to make ends meet. Some people ended up losing their homes. Although some people caught COVID and survived, others caught the virus and struggled to return to normal.

Even during a global pandemic, we are called to obey Saint Paul's command, "Rejoice always; pray without ceasing; in everything give thanks; for this is God's will for you in Christ Jesus."[69] Saint Paul wrote his first epistle to the church in Thessalonica around 50-51 A.D.[70] Orthodox Christians remain people of joy regardless of the circumstances. Saint Paul endured house arrest around 61-63 A.D., a few years prior to his martyrdom, while he shared these words in his epistle to the church in Philippi, "Rejoice in the Lord always. Again I will say, rejoice!"[71] Saint Paul wrote these two passages challenging us to rejoice regardless of our circumstances in the Greek imperative; as such, his words are a strong command, not a mere suggestion. Saints Peter and Paul faced death with courage and grace. "Exactly how long the two Apostles languished in prison is not known. But most writers believe that it was sometime during the summer of A.D. 67 when Paul of Tarsus was finally roused from his coal-black cell and taken, blinking in the sun, to a lonely spot along the Ostian Way for execution."[72] Like Saint Paul, we too must rejoice, regardless of our circumstances, even in the midst of a global pandemic.

To one degree or another, we all were forced to accept a certain degree of solitude during this treacherous time. Sick people died alone. Faced with a lockdown, many people ex-

---

[69] 1 Thessalonians 5:16-18 NASB.

[70] *The Orthodox Study Bible: New Testament and Psalms, New King James Version* (Nashville, TN: Thomas Nelson Publishers, 1993), 470.

[71] Philippians 4:4 NKJV.

[72] Rod Bennett, *Four Witnesses: The Early Church in Her Own Words* (San Francisco: Ignatius Press, 2002), 77.

perienced acute loneliness. Even within families, there was a forced distancing and separation. Some churches closed their doors and invited their parishioners to try to worship online. Many students learned with the computer rather than within the classroom. The global pandemic brought sickness and death, fear and solitude.

Faced with this stark reality, people were offered a clear choice. We were not free to shape our circumstances. Yet we were free to choose under the pressure of a global pandemic and forced lockdowns whether to get bitter or better. There are continual choices throughout our life journey: Will we face challenging circumstances with courage or cowardice? When something bad happens, do we get better or bitter? Do we follow the lead of Saint Paul and rejoice or walk the way of the world towards despair? Whenever solitude is thrust upon us, beyond our control, it is critical to celebrate rather than scorn these unexpected life upheavals.

Monks and nuns laboring in monasteries and hermitages around the globe celebrate solitude better than anyone I know. "Let it not be hidden from beloved brethren that the highest kinds of monastic life–that is to say, solitude in a remote desert or silence in reclusion, or living with a Spirit-bearing elder in unconditional obedience to him–were not established by chance, or by the will and intelligence of man, but by the special providence, design, vocation, and revelation of God."[73] Although God calls some men and women to embrace monasticism, all of us are called and challenged to celebrate solitude whenever it arrives at our doorsteps.

----

[73] Bishop Ignatius Brianchaninov, *The Arena: Guidelines for Spiritual and Monastic Life* (Jordanville, NY: Holy Trinity Publications, 2012), 25.

By squarely facing and successfully overcoming this challenge, faithful monks and nuns fulfilling their vows with integrity and grace serve as our guides. We may be better able to learn how to celebrate solitude with their able assistance.

"The monk is a Christian who has responded to a special call from God, and has withdrawn from the more active concerns of a worldly life, in order to devote himself completely to repentance, 'conversion,' *metanoia*, renunciation and prayer."[74] Each of these ascetical approaches draw us closer to God. "For whosoever will save his life shall lose it, and whosoever will lose his life for my sake shall find it."[75] The main mission of the monastery is powerful prayer, an assignment all Christians accept. Our people in the pews, our readers and acolytes, our magnificent chanters and choirs, our subdeacons and deacons, our priests and bishops, all of us are called by God to seek union with Him through intimate prayer as we strive to "pray without ceasing."[76]

The Divine Office nurtures this communion with God. At Saint Patrick Orthodox Church in Virginia, our Western Rite Parish prays the Divine Office using *The Monastic Diurnal*, a powerful resource offering the "Day Hours of the Monastic Breviary According to the Holy Rule of Saint Benedict."[77] For the Desert Fathers, love for God "expressed itself first of all in love for God's Word. Prayer was drawn from the Scriptures, especially from the Psalms. The first monks looked upon the Psalter not only as a kind of compendium of all the other

---

[74] Thomas Merton, *Contemplative Prayer*, 19.

[75] Matthew 16:25 KJV.

[76] 1 Thessalonians 5:17 NKJV.

[77] *The Monastic Diurnal* (London: Oxford University Press, 1963), iii.

books of the Bible, but as a book of special efficacy for the ascetic life, in that it revealed the secret movements of the heart in its struggle against the forces of darkness."[78]

Monastic prayer has a rich and ancient history. "The Monastic Office was first set forth in all of its essential features and in much of its detail about the year 535 A.D. in the Holy Rule of St. Benedict, the father of Western monasticism. It was the first complete and enduring order of daily praise and prayer in European Christendom. For fourteen hundred years it has voiced the worship of an ever-increasing circle of devout men and women."[79] At the heart of monastic life is the chanting of the Psalms. " 'Sing the psalms with understanding', says the psalmist (Ps. 47 : 7); and the Lord says, 'Search the Scriptures' (John 5 : 39). He who pays attention to them is illumined, while he who pays no attention is filled with darkness. For unless a person attends to what is said in divine Scripture, he will gather but little fruit, even though he sings or reads them frequently."[80]

When faced with solitude, it is critical to pray. Imagine the hundreds and thousands of hours and millions of minutes humanity wasted worrying about a global pandemic beyond our control. What if all that lost time could have been replaced with reliance on these words of Saint Paul, again in the Greek imperative? "Do not be anxious about anything, but in everything by prayer and pleading with thanksgiving

---

[78] Thomas Merton, *Contemplative Prayer*, 20.

[79] *The Monastic Diurnal*, v.

[80] Saint Peter of Damaskos, "Twenty-Four Discourses," *The Philokalia*, vol. 3, compiled by Saint Nikodemos and Saint Makarios, translated and edited by G.E.H. Palmer, Philip Sherrard, and Kallistos Ware (New York: Faber and Faber, 1984), 263-264.

let your requests be made known to God."[81] Faced with a forced solitude, wouldn't prayer and thanks have served us better than worry and anxiety? "If you patiently accept what comes, you will always pray with joy."[82] The end result of a holy solitude is epic: "And the peace of God, which surpasses all comprehension, will guard your hearts and minds in Christ Jesus."[83]

---

[81] Philippians 4:6 NASB.

[82] Evagrios the Solitary, "On Prayer: One Hundred and Fifty-Three Texts," *The Philokalia*, vol. 1, 59.

[83] Philippians 4:7 NASB.

CHAPTER FOUR

ESSENTIAL EMPTINESS

Let nothing *be done* through selfish ambition or conceit, but in lowliness of mind let each esteem others better than himself. Let each of you look out not only for his own interests, but also for the interests of others. Let this mind be in you which was also in Christ Jesus, who, being in the form of God, did not consider it robbery to be equal with God, but made Himself of no reputation, taking the form of a bondservant, *and* coming in the likeness of men (Philippians 2:3-7 NKJV).

After growing up Roman Catholic in the State of Indiana, attending Saint Charles Borromeo Grade School, Bishop Dwenger High School, and the University of Notre Dame, I began my teaching and coaching career at Catholic schools. Nearly three decades ago, I served as the co-chair of the Parish Council at Holy Name Church while teaching fifth grade at Risen Christ School in South Minneapolis. Located between my inner-city church and school was the intersection of 38th Street and Chicago Avenue, the site where nearly fifteen years later on Monday 25 May 2020, after the lockdowns and in the midst of the global pandemic, George Floyd was murdered.

I taught and coached at this superb inner-city school with much joy and purpose. During this time, I earned a Master's degree in Elementary Education with a focus on Students-at-Risk, and what I learned during Weekend College at the College of Saint Catherine in Saint Paul was brought with much benefit immediately into my fifth-grade classroom and while coaching basketball, soccer, and wrestling. There were challenges during these first years of my career as an educator. One eighth-grade student at our school was shot by a stray bullet and remains paralyzed to this day. I lived in South Minneapolis for six years, and although I felt safe, you had to be careful.

I especially recall one typical Tuesday. Three teachers including myself unlocked our cars in the parking lot at nearly the same time at the end of an ordinary school day. I was in the middle car as we entered the street. As we approached the stoplight at 38th and Portland, two of us made it through the green and yellow lights, respectively, past Chicago Avenue, while one teacher stopped on the red. My first colleague kept going straight on 38th Street, I turned and entered the highway for the long trek to teach a Business Law evening course at Anoka-Ramsey Community College, and the third teacher waited at the red light. She noticed something unusual, one man chasing another, and soon both men ran closer and closer to the intersection. All of a sudden, a gunshot was fired, and the back windshield of this teacher's car was shattered by the stray bullet. Although she was unhurt, as I drove her to school the next week while her car was in the shop, this friend asked me to take a slight detour and avoid the intersection of 38th and Portland.

My time at this excellent Roman Catholic School in South Minneapolis brought far much more joy than sorrow. My fifth-grade scholars actually wrote books of different lengths, some typed and others handwritten, their longest novel close to one hundred pages. I still have many of these books today. Many years later, one of my former students as an adult asked me to officiate as the minister of his wedding. I love to visit the Twin Cities and still have many lifelong friends there.

The most tragic memory of my inner-city teaching experience occurred a few years after I left the area and moved to Virginia. While home from college during a school break, one of my former fifth-graders, actually named in my Elementary Education Master's thesis, was shot and killed. During the Canon of the Mass each Sunday and Feast Day, we pause to pray for both the living and the dead. As we pray for the living, I recall my family and friends. As we pray for the dead, besides my deceased family members, I remember two influential Roman Catholic priests, Fathers Walter Dolan and Zachary Hayes of blessed memory, two Orthodox priests leading me into Orthodoxy, Fathers Peter Gillquist and Alexander Atty of blessed memory, Metropolitan Kallistos Ware recently falling asleep, two wonder-filled nuns Mother Sophia and Mother Olga of blessed memory, the deceased son of a friend, and three former students facing untimely deaths, including this former fifth-grade student shot to death in Minneapolis.

Death brings an unbridled emptiness into our hearts. When faced with our own inevitable death or the sickness and death brutalizing those we love, we answer these challenges deep down inside, in a place of lonely and special solitude. It is here amidst the sorrow of tragedy that we decide whether to get bitter or better.

Saint Symeon the New Theologian lived during the turn of the first millennium. He "taught the sublimity of self-abasement and the sure proof of perfect love" by inviting his readers to "experience the richness of God's condescension and know the gift of His great and inexhaustible self-emptying for us *(Phil. 2:7)*. Learn in how awesome a manner our earthly [being] is re-created, and how those men live who have consented to believe in Christ crucified, that is, those who imitate His obedience and self-abasement and desire to turn from evil to good."[84] Jesus as the Son of God is 100% divine; Jesus as the Son of Man is 100% human. Fully God, Jesus "did not lose what he was but kept his unchangeable nature, and was ever established in the highest dignity of godhead"[85] and declared, "I and *my* Father are one."[86] Fully human, Jesus endured human suffering and embraced our death. "Even though he is equal to God the Father, he obediently endured the sufferings and the cross. Because all these things were part and parcel of the human condition he adopted them as being implied along with the flesh, and so he fulfilled the economy, though always remaining what he was."[87]

In order to pray effectively, we must walk in the footprints of the Master and continually strive to empty ourselves. A monk embraces emptiness not as an end in itself but as a means to the end. "In positive terms, we must understand the monastic life above all as a life of prayer. The negative elements, solitude, fasting, obedience, penance, renunciation of property and of ambition, are all intended to clear the way so that prayer, meditation and contemplation may fill the space

---

[84] Symeon the New Theologian, *The Discourses*, translated by C.J. deCatanzaro (Mahwah, NJ: Paulist Press, 1980), 207.

[85] John McGuckin, *Saint Cyril of Alexandria and the Christological Controversy* (Crestwood, NY: St. Vladimir's Seminary Press, 1995), 321.

[86] John 10:30 KJV.

[87] John McGuckin, *Saint Cyril of Alexandria and the Christological Controversy*, 298.

created by the abandonment of other concerns."[88] Although the pathway to holiness is cleared and made straighter by what we do, real transformational change of the heart happens when we look deep down inside. To effectuate change and walk closer to God, we need to look beyond the surface and seek a changed heart.

"Enter ye in at the strait gate: for wide *is* the gate, and broad *is* the way, that leadeth to destruction, and many there be which go in thereat: Because strait *is* the gate, and narrow *is* the way, which leadeth unto life, and few there be that find it."[89] We find the narrow gate by not only renouncing things on the outside, but even more relevantly, by facing temptation and combatting sin within ourselves. "This gateway is opened only by emptying ourselves of those things to which we are only too ready to be enslaved; not, as some would think, the material things we must properly use to transform our world into a more perfect one but our selfishness, arrogance, bitterness–our gold–which serve to close us off from the other trying to enter."[90]

There are two divergent paths to embrace our inevitable emptiness. We must first work diligently to replace pride with humility. We then must act in love.

"For all that *is* in the world–the lust of the flesh, the lust of the eyes, and the pride of life–is not of the Father but is of the world."[91] Archimandrite Sophrony, the spiritual disciple of Saint Silouan of Mount Athos, presents a sterling summary of pride as the source of all sin and suffering along a continuum, small to great:

---

[88] Thomas Merton, *Contemplative Prayer*, 19.

[89] Matthew 7:13-14 KJV.

[90] Metropolitan Philip Saliba and Joseph J. Allen, *Meeting the Incarnate God*, 27.

[91] 1 John 2:16 NKJV.

> Pride is the source of sin, comprising every aspect that evil can assume – conceit, ambition, indifference, cruelty, disregard of the suffering of others; day-dreaming, over-fantasising, a demented expression in the eye, in every other feature; gloom, melancholy, despair, animosity; envy, an inferiority complex, carnal desires; wearisome psychological disturbances, rebellious feelings, fear of death or, on the contrary, wanting to put an end to life; and, lastly and not seldom, utter madness. These are the indications of demonic spirituality. But until they show up quickly, they pass unnoticed by many.[92]

The pride of life, the source of sin. Compare and contrast our most entrenched sin with the essential emptiness embraced by Jesus Christ, God yet man, from heaven to earth, from Christmas Joy to the Calvary Cross. "He, indeed, assumed humanity that we might become God."[93]

Besides facing our inherent pride and seeking to nurture humility within our hearts, we may try to connect this newfound humility with concrete actions loving and serving both God and neighbor. To attack their vices, monks strive to "forget themselves and apply themselves entirely to the love and service of God."[94] As Jesus told the lawyer tempting Him, "Thou shalt love the Lord thy God with all thy heart, and with all thy soul, and with all thy mind. This is the first and great commandment. And the second *is* like

---

[92] Archimandrite Sophrony, *Saint Silouan the Athonite*, translated by Rosemary Edmonds (Crestwood, NY: St. Vladimir's Seminary Press, 1991), 203-204.

[93] Saint Athanasius, *On the Incarnation* (Crestwood, NY: St. Vladimir's Seminary Press, 1996), 93.

[94] Thomas Merton, *Contemplative Prayer*, 20.

unto it, Thou shalt love thy neighbour as thyself. On these two commandments hang all the law and the prophets."[95] To love God, we need to empty our hearts, souls, and minds of anything and everything separating us from Him. "St. John Climacus speaks of our love of God as 'passionate': 'Blessed is the person whose desire for God has become like the lover's passion for the beloved.' St. Maximus the Confessor called our relationship with God *eros maniakos*, a deeply erotic relationship of love."[96] To serve God, we need to not only love our neighbor as much as we love ourselves, we also must love our enemies: "Ye have heard that it hath been said, Thou shalt love thy neighbour, and hate thine enemy. But I say unto you, Love your enemies, bless them that curse you, do good to them that hate you, and pray for them which despitefully use you and persecute you; That ye may be the children of your Father which is in heaven."[97]

Imagine the joy emanating from our lives, a joy overflowing from our hearts, were we truly able to empty ourselves and replace all the stuff we now hold so dear with the powerful presence of Jesus. Within each human being, there is a choice to live our days with either the false self of the world or our true self in Christ. Pursuing the narrow way of Christ by accepting our own emptiness is worth the price.

....

[95] Matthew 22:37-40 KJV.

[96] Anthony M. Conairis, *God and You: Person to Person* (Minneapolis, MN: Light & Life Publishing, 2005), 15.

[97] Matthew 5:43-45a KJV.

CHAPTER FIVE

EMBRACING LONELINESS

And being found in appearance as a man, He humbled Himself and became obedient to *the point of* death, even the death of the cross. Therefore God also has highly exalted Him and given Him the name which is above every name, that at the name of Jesus every knee should bow, of those in heaven, and of those on earth, and of those under the earth, and *that* every tongue should confess that Jesus Christ *is* Lord, to the glory of God the Father (Philippians 2:8-11 NKJV).

Jesus the Crucified Christ willingly welcomed and freely embraced the stark loneliness of the Cross. "He became a slave for us even to the point of washing our feet and dying the death of a slave on the cross for our sins."[98] Even when surrounded by family and friends, all of humanity dies alone. This ultimate, utter loneliness is most clearly seen with the Cross of Christ at Calvary, the Son of God at Golgatha. The Blessed Virgin Mary, Saint John the Apostle, and Mary Magdalene were among those standing and praying with Jesus on the Cross. Although they suffered with Christ, Jesus as fully human walked the lonely road from life to death alone and by Himself.

---

[98] Anthony M. Conairis, *God and You: Person to Person*, 44.

I held Dad's hand as he breathed his last nearly four decades ago. I was with him, by his bedside, yet I am convinced his walk from life to death was a lonely walk. We all die alone. The Crucified Christ shows us how to embrace even the starkest loneliness with courage and grace.

Death takes two forms, both spiritual and physical. Although we often focus upon our inevitable physical death, infinitely more pertinent is to fear our possible spiritual death. "Death has both a physical and spiritual aspect, and of the two it is the spiritual that is the most terrible. Physical death is the separation of man's body from his soul; spiritual death, the separation of man's soul from God."[99] The wrenching away of the soul from the body epitomizes the loneliness of physical death. Yet an even more lonely and challenging journey occurs were we to be spiritually estranged from God after our physical death. Throughout our life, each of us is called upon to "work out your own salvation with fear and trembling."[100] Death surrounds our desire for salvation. Jesus shows us the way to embrace the loneliness inherent in death.

"When we say that Christ became 'obedient unto death' (Phil. 2:8), we are not to limit these words to physical death alone. We should not think only of the bodily sufferings which Christ endured at his Passion–the scourging, the stumbling beneath the weight of the Cross, the nails, the thirst and heat, the torment of hanging stretched on the wood. The true meaning of the Passion is found, not in this only, but much more in his spiritual suffering–in his sense of failure, isolation, and utter loneliness, in the pain of love offered

---

[99] Bishop Kallistos Ware, *The Orthodox Way*, 79.
[100] Philippians 2:12b NKJV.

but rejected."[101] In a similar way, we suffer throughout life both physically and spiritually. We suffer physically when sicknesses from cancer to COVID wrack our body with indescribable pain. We suffer emotionally when battling despair and depression. Yet even more pronounced, even more painful, is when we suffer spiritually by freely choosing to sin.

Monks and nuns understand both spiritual and physical death uniquely. "True monasticism is invisible martyrdom."[102] Saint Antony, the founder of monasticism, was about nineteen years old when he went to church one day nearly six months after his parents died. Along the way he walked and considered "how the apostles, forsaking everything, followed the Savior."[103] He reflected upon how in the early Church there was no one "among them who lacked; for all who were possessors of lands or houses sold them, and brought the proceeds of the things that were sold, and laid *them* at the apostles' feet; and they distributed to each as anyone had need."[104] His heart may have soared as he realized "great hope is stored up for such people in heaven (footnote 5: Mt. 4:20; Acts 4:35; Mt. 19:21). He went into the church pondering these things, and just then it happened that the Gospel was being read, and he heard the Lord saying to the rich man, *If you would be perfect, go, sell what you possess and give to the poor, and you will have treasure in heaven* (footnote 6: Mt. 19:21). It was as if by God's design he held the saints in his recollection, and as if the passage were read on his account. Immediately Antony

---

[101] Bishop Kallistos Ware, *The Orthodox Way*, 79.

[102] Bishop Ignatius Brianchaninov, *The Arena: Guidelines for Spiritual and Monastic Life*, 178.

[103] Athanasius, *The Life of Antony and the Letter to Marcellinus*, translated by Robert C. Gregg (Mahwah, NJ: Paulist Press, 1980), 31.

[104] Acts 4:34-35 NKJV.

went out from the Lord's house and gave to the townspeople the possessions he had from his forebears."[105] Unlike myself upon hearing in homilies hundreds of Scriptural examples, Saint Antony truly followed this command of Saint James: "Don't I beg you, only hear the message, but put it into practice; otherwise you are merely deluding yourselves."[106] Saint Antony not only heard the Word of God, he welcomed the Word into his heart and acted immediately.

Jesus taught His disciples how to pray, and in that precise instruction, we pray the Lord's Prayer, the Our Father, during the Divine Liturgy and the Divine Office. "*Our Father in heaven, may your name be hallowed, your Kingdom come, your will be done on earth as it is in heaven. Give us today our daily bread, and forgive us our debts, as we forgive our debtors; and do not lead us into temptation, but deliver us from the evil one.*"[107] Jesus showed us how to seek to discover and strive to follow the will of God the Father. "I can of mine own self do nothing: as I hear, I judge: and my judgment is just; because I seek not mine own will, but the will of the Father which hath sent me."[108] After the Last Supper, Jesus prayed with a fervent intensity in the Garden of Gethsemane at the Mount of Olives. Abandoned by His sleeping disciples, Jesus embraced loneliness in the depth of suffering. "And he was withdrawn from them about a stone's cast, and kneeled down, and prayed, Saying, Father, if thou be willing, remove this cup from me: nevertheless, not my will,

....

[105] Athanasius, *The Life of Antony and the Letter to Marcellinus*, 31.

[106] James 1:22 Phillips Modern English.

[107] Hieromonk Gregorios, *The Divine Liturgy: A Commentary in the Light of the Fathers* (Mount Athos Koutloumousiou Monastery, Greece: Cell of St John the Theologian, 2009), 263.

[108] John 5:30 KJV.

but thine, be done. And there appeared an angel unto him from heaven, strengthening him. And being in an agony he prayed more earnestly: and his sweat was as it were great drops of blood falling down to the ground."[109] Following the holy will of His heavenly Father, Jesus became obedient, even willingly walking towards a most painful and horrific crucifixion.

What is the will of God? Saint Cyprian, the third-century bishop of Carthage, offers an answer in reflecting upon the Lord's Prayer:

> Now the will of God is that which Christ both did and taught. Humility in conduct, constancy in faith, truth in speech, justice in deeds, mercy in works, restraint in self-discipline, knowing nothing of doing injury yet willing to endure slight, holding to peace with the brothers, devoted wholeheartedly to the Lord, loving him as Father, fearing him as God, preferring nothing whatsoever to Christ because he preferred nothing to ourselves, clinging inseparably to his love, standing by his cross with courage and faith, and, when his name and honor are contested, being a confessor by constancy in what we say, being defiant by fidelity under interrogation, receiving the crown by patience under sentence of death. This is the desire to be co-heir with Christ, this is the performance of the command of God, this is the fulfillment of the will of God.[110]

---

[109] Luke 22:41-44 KJV.

[110] Cyprian, *On the Lord's Prayer: Tertullian, Cyprian, Origen*, translated by Alistair Stewart-Sykes (Crestwood, NY: St. Vladimir's Seminary Press, 2004), 75-76.

An unwavering, single-minded devotion to the will of God is required. "Blessed *are* the pure in heart: for they shall see God."[111] Saint Antony "endeavored each day to present himself as the sort of person ready to appear before God–that is, pure of heart and prepared to obey his will, and no other."[112] The Holy Trinity – God the Father, God the Son, God the Holy Spirit – has been, is, and always will be uncreated. We forever will be created. In order to obey the will of Our Father, and no other, we as created beings must be willing to embrace the loneliness inherent within our human nature.

Our ultimate loneliness occurs on our deathbed. There simply is no escaping death. We all shall die. Each day we awaken and find ourselves one step closer to death. Our daily trek towards the grave seems both gradual and invisible yet is both apparent and inevitable. We actually die a little each and every day. Understanding these daily deaths helps us comprehend and appreciate the inherent loneliness of our everyday lives.

On a positive note, God calls us to die a little each day to our own desires as we choose instead to seek His will. God is uncreated, we are created, and the gap is infinite. Yet we walk upward towards heaven to the extent we climb the Cross of Christ towards God. "When we are called by God to various renunciations and 'deaths' so that we can experience the corresponding resurrections, we must not lose heart so that we can climb up high. To go backwards, or even to stand still, means falling."[113] Saint Paul lived a lonely life enriched

---

[111] Matthew 5:8 KJV.

[112] Athanasius, *The Life of Antony and the Letter to Marcellinus*, 37.

[113] Metropolitan of Nafpaktos Hierotheos, *Hesychia and Theology: The Context for Man's Healing in the Orthodox Church*, translated by Sister Pelagia Selfe (Levadia, Greece: Birth of the Theotokos Monastery,

by the Cross of Christ. "I am crucified with Christ: nevertheless I live; yet not I, but Christ liveth in me: and the life which I now live in the flesh I live by the faith of the Son of God, who loved me, and gave himself for me."[114] The critical key unlocking the door to a joyful embrace of loneliness is discoverable in the Cross of Christ.

My most influential, life-changing, lifelong-learning course taken at the University of Notre Dame more than four decades ago was called Theology and Community Service. This class brought about a dozen students into a local nursing home. The course was team-taught by Father Don McNeill and Sister Vivian Whitehead. The main theme of this course is summarized best by this short passage from a now-published draft manuscript serving as our textbook: "Compassion asks us to go where it hurts, to enter into places of pain, to share in brokenness, fear, confusion, and anguish. Compassion challenges us to cry out with those in misery, to mourn with those who are lonely, to weep with those in tears. Compassion requires us to be weak with the weak, vulnerable with the vulnerable, and powerless with the powerless. Compassion means full immersion in the condition of being human."[115]

Each student was assigned two elderly nursing home residents. We would see them weekly during this semester course with back-to-back visits of forty-five minutes. I visited Iris and Joe at a South Bend, Indiana, nursing home. I still recall the potent smell of decay as I walked through the front door to begin my first two visits. I walked into Joe's room first as he sat on the edge of his bed in a dark

---

2007), 91.

[114] Galatians 2:20 KJV.

[115] Henri J. M. Nouwen, Donald P. McNeill, and Douglas A. Morrison, *Compassion* (New York: Doubleday, 1982), 4.

and gloomy room. I vividly recall his litany of complaints against the nursing home and its staff. Joe hated living at the institution, the staff treated the residents "like dirt," and the food was like garbage, the meals so disgusting he would not feed them "to the pigs." Generally optimistic, even overly so, nothing I could say helped break the gloom and doom surrounding our first conversation.

After this somewhat depressing visit, I walked down the hallway and entered Iris' brightly-lit room. A cheerful woman, Iris loved the Lord and enthusiastically talked about Jesus. I especially recall a life-size glass dog she enjoyed as if it were a real pet. After listening to Joe's harangue, I sheepishly asked Iris about her experiences. Unlike Joe, Iris loved the nursing home. The nurses and orderlies treated the residents "like kings and queens." Every meal was like "a feast." When hit with hard times as a young woman, at a point of near despair, doing dishes at the kitchen sink many years ago, Iris looked outside the window and suddenly received the insight, "There's always darkness before the dawn." She laughed at once and overcame her sadness at the time and instead felt immense joy. Since that religious experience many years earlier, Iris' life was transformed towards the good, and she was never the same.

I began writing extensively in a journal during my semester-long nursing home visits and completed close to two dozen journals throughout my early adult years. A recurring theme permeating my first journal in this Theology and Community Service course was loneliness. Here was a Labor Day entry penned near the beginning of my pivotal Senior Year at Notre Dame:

> No matter how close we are to other people, we are all unique individuals: we enter this earth as independent

beings and will leave it in exactly the same manner. Rather than scorn this basic loneliness, treasure it – our independence is the foundation of one's beautiful uniqueness. Although we need the help of others to nurture and grow, we also need a healthy sense of self-esteem which recognizes the fundamental entity that is "me." Strive toward a proper degree of self-reliance by asserting your own independence, the foundation of each person's special goodness.[116]

Sister Vivian offered insightful instructional comments in the margin of my collegiate journal in response to this entry. She asked how we can learn to treasure loneliness and shared how it is "the love and friendship of others that helps us appreciate ourselves."[117] Besides the joy of love and friendship, there are two powerful ways to both accept and alleviate our inevitable loneliness. We embrace loneliness to the extent we fill our hearts with a deep and abiding love for the Trinity and the Theotokos. We partially alleviate the pain of loneliness to the extent we share the Cross of Christ by entering into the pain of others.

It is only through the suffering of the Cross of Christ that we can both share the pain and ease the loneliness of others. "In theology, *compassion* means that the sufferer is 'grasped' by one who 'co-passionates'."[118] To be compassionate to-

---

[116] David Lochbihler, 4 September 1978, "Independence Theory," Theology and Community Service, University of Notre Dame, Notre Dame, IN, Journal Entry.

[117] Sister Vivian Whitehead, 6 September 1978, Theology and Community Service, University of Notre Dame, Notre Dame, IN, Journal Comment.

[118] Allen, *Inner Way*, 83 (emphasis in original).

wards others, we must be in touch with our own suffering. By "remaining in touch with his own experiences of suffering, sinfulness, and limitations,"[119] a servant walks hand-in-hand with the wounded into the places of pain together. The wounded one no longer faces suffering alone. To enter the places of pain and truly listen to and experience the suffering shared by others, we need to be in touch with our own pain and suffering. Within a therapeutic context, "*empathy* helps healing to occur because the patient feels that his or her counselor is truly capable of entering his frame and perspective."[120] Although we can never understand fully another person's unique experience of pain and suffering, our ability to empathize with others is enhanced to the degree we have faced and accepted our own pain and suffering. By becoming one of us and dying on the Cross, Jesus offered humanity the ability to once again be reborn in the image and likeness of God through the power of love.

By loving and living for God, we may replace the emptiness of death with hope. "Happiness is not something that you can do, but it will rather just be if you care and love others. If we care for others, we can overcome loneliness in this life. To cope with death, with the emptiness which it emits from the dying, we must care not only for others but for God. If death is to be the fulfillment of our lives rather than an emptiness staring at the unknown, we must seek out the unknown through God."[121] Sister Vivian aptly describes how overcoming suffering parallels the journey from death to

---

[119] Ibid.

[120] Ibid (emphasis in original).

[121] David Lochbihler, 25 September 1978, Theology and Community Service, University of Notre Dame, Notre Dame, IN, Journal Entry (emphasis in original).

eternal life: "John Dunne speaks of death as a passing through to greater life. Maybe we can understand this a little from our human experience of suffering something and knowing that we passed through that suffering to a deeper growth and life in ourselves."[122]

By loving our neighbor, we in fact catch a glimpse of God. Whatever our vocation, we move closer to the holiness of our Triune God to the extent we strive to love God and love our neighbor in everything we do. "You can't care for God in a vacuum, but only through other people with whom we fulfil the mission of love on earth."[123] We love God to the extent we love our neighbor: "Come, ye blessed of my Father, inherit the kingdom prepared for you from the foundation of the world: For I was a hungered, and ye gave me meat: I was thirsty, and ye gave me drink: I was a stranger, and ye took me in: Naked, and ye clothed me: I was sick, and ye visited me: I was in prison, and ye came unto me."[124]

"To care for people is to share their joy and sorrow, their hope and despair, their triumph and defeat."[125] I have felt a deep and abiding call to the priesthood since fourth grade. At the heart of my vocation is a lifelong quest to embrace loneliness in my life, especially the loneliness of celibacy, as an avenue enhancing my ability to love: "When I accept my own loneliness, I am at once united with <u>literally all of hu-</u>

---

[122] Sister Vivian Whitehead, 28 September 1978, Theology and Community Service, University of Notre Dame, Notre Dame, IN, Journal Comment.

[123] David Lochbihler, 25 September 1978, Theology and Community Service, University of Notre Dame, Notre Dame, IN, Journal Entry.

[124] Matthew 25:34b-36 KJV.

[125] Joseph J. Allen, ed., *And He Leads Them* (Ben Lomond, CA: Conciliar Press, 2001), 244.

manity. Only then am I able to live a truly complete human life."[126] As I reflect on my past pastoral ministry experiences and discern God's call in my life, these words of His Eminence Metropolitan Philip of thrice-blessed memory are most inspiring: "Priesthood is not a job; it is a *vocation*. Priesthood is not a profession; it is a covenant between the priest and his parish."[127] Just as the incarnate Christ was fully God and fully man, both God and bondservant, so too are we called to bring the light of Jesus our God into the hearts of hurting people, uniting the divine with the human. The Priest's mission is to lead His people to Jesus Christ. As Metropolitan Philip directed his Priests, "You were ordained in order to bring Christ to people and people to Christ."[128]

All Christians assume a similar priestly presence within our lives as we love and serve one another. "But ye are a chosen generation, a royal priesthood, an holy nation, a peculiar people; that ye should shew forth the praises of him who hath called you out of darkness into his marvelous light."[129] Whatever our vocational call from God, we shall face loneliness, and strengthened by our Orthodox faith, we may work through this loneliness and emerge from darkness into the light of Christ.

....

[126] David Lochbihler, 6 October 1978, Theology and Community Service, University of Notre Dame, Notre Dame, IN, Journal Entry (emphasis in original).

[127] Joseph J. Allen, ed., *And He Leads Them*, 244 (emphasis in original).

[128] Joseph J. Allen, ed., *Orthodox Synthesis: The Unity of Theological Thought* (Crestwood, NY: St. Vladimir's Seminary Press, 1981), 95.

[129] 1 Peter 2:9 KJV.

CHAPTER SIX

STILL SILENCE

> My soul, wait silently for God alone,
> For my expectation *is* from Him
> He only *is* my rock and my salvation;
> *He* is my defense;
> I shall not be moved.
> In God *is* my salvation and my glory;
> The rock of my strength,
> *And* my refuge, *is* in God
> (Psalm 62:5-7 NKJV).

God is everywhere. Prayerfully wondering about the omniscience, omnipotence, and immutability of God, we strive to discover Him through the mighty magnificence of His creation.

> And he said, Go forth, and stand upon the mount before the LORD. And, behold, the LORD passed by, and a great and strong wind rent the mountains, and brake in pieces the rocks before the LORD; but the LORD was not in the wind: and after the wind an earthquake; but the LORD was not in the earthquake: And after the earthquake a fire; but the LORD was not in the fire.[130]

---

[130] 1 Kings 19:11-12a KJV.

The Prophet Elijah could not find God in the largest and most powerful elements of wind, earthquake, and fire. We tend with our pride to mold God in our created image rather than with humility bend ourselves and our human will toward His uncreated image. Because of this, we focus far too much upon the externals rather than what is truly important in life. Before we even begin to try to discover God, we must realize "man looketh on the outward appearance, but the LORD looketh on the heart."[131]

Elijah could better appreciate the power and presence of God surrounding him once his mind shifted from the grandiose creation to the possibility of a smaller yet more real truth.

> To see a World in a grain of sand,
> And a Heaven in a wild flower,
> Hold Infinity in the palm of your hand,
> And Eternity in an hour.[132]

By pausing to ponder the simple, the prophet discovered God not in the mighty forces of nature but rather by hearkening his heart towards "a still small voice."[133]

We experience still silence best amidst the mystery of our Orthodox Divine Liturgy. "When the faithful attend a service to praise God, they come into contact with the Bible's treasures and relate to them, as the Fathers of the Church decreed."[134]

---

[131] 1 Samuel 16:7 KJV.

[132] William Blake, "Auguries of Innocence," *The Poetical Works of William Blake*, ed. John Sampson (London: Oxford University, 1934), 171.

[133] 1 Kings 19:12b KJV.

[134] Metropolitan of Nafpaktos Hierotheos, *Hesychia and Theology:*

Serving as a Deacon in the Orthodox Church brings great joy to my heart. Each Sunday prior to Mass at Saint Patrick Orthodox Church, I like to unlock the door earlier than anyone, hoping to be the first to arrive in the still silence of a fresh dawning Sunday. There are many chores to perform. Before doing anything, it is important to enter the Sanctuary and acknowledge the power and presence of Almighty God, the Blessed Virgin Mary, and all the Saints and Angels. I genuflect before the Tabernacle containing the Body and Blood of Christ. Behind the Holy Altar are four magnificent icons: Saint Patrick, our patron saint; the Incarnation, the Theotokos with the Child Jesus; Christ the Teacher; and Saint John the Baptist. Every minute of every day, a great cloud of witnesses surrounds our Holy Altar. Preparing for Mass is a wonderful opportunity to simply stand and serve in the Presence of God.

My first chore, to be done once a week, is to light the Vigil Candle. The Body of Christ within the Tabernacle never sits in complete darkness, even at the stroke of midnight during the blackest of nights. A few steps up the ladder, I remove the old candle nearly spent from the mild steel ceiling holder and light a long taper to transfer the old flame onto the new candle. After performing such a noble task, I place this lit taper in the sand in the brass bowl at the back of church to light the few candles still with wick and to join the other candles soon-to-be lit by the faithful as they enter the Church to worship. Although my entire weekly ritual with the lit taper is not necessary, I find prayerfully completing these additional few steps enhances the beauty and solemnity of this simple task.

The Context for Man's Healing in the Orthodox Church, 181.

Another chore is to lay out Father's Vestments in the Sacristy. This sacred apparel is laid from bottom to top, enabling Father to prepare for Lauds and Mass by vesting with one item at a time. While washing his hands, Father prays, "Cleanse my hands, O Lord, from all stain, that, pure in mind and body, I may be worthy to serve thee." Father places the Amice upon his head and prays, "Place, O Lord, the helmet of Salvation upon my head to repel the assaults of the Devil." While putting on the Alb, Father prays, "Cleanse me, O Lord, and purify my heart, that, being made white in the Blood of the Lamb, I may attain everlasting joy." While tying the Cincture upon his waist, Father prays, "Gird me, O Lord, with the girdle of purity and quench in me the fire of concupiscence, that the grace of temperance and chastity may abide in me." The Maniple, used at Mass and not during Lauds, is placed on the left arm with the prayer, "Grant me, O Lord, to bear the light burden of grief and sorrow, that I may with gladness take the reward of my labor." The Holy Stole worn by Priests and Deacons is placed around the neck with this solemn prayer, "Give me again, O Lord, the stole of immortality, which I lost by the transgression of my first parents, and although I am unworthy to come unto Thy Holy Sacrament, grant that I may attain everlasting felicity." With the Deacon donning the Dalmatic and the Subdeacon wearing the Tunicle, Father places the opening of the Chasuble past his head and upon his shoulders with this final prayer of preparation, "Lord, who has said, My yoke is easy, and My burden is light, grant that I may so bear it, as to attain Thy grace. Amen."[135] As the Deacon lays the Vestments in the

---

[135] "The Prayers to be Said While Vesting," Saint Patrick Orthodox Church Sacristy, from Dom Gaspar Lefebvre, *The Saint Andrew Daily Missal* (Great Falls, MT: St. Bonaventure Publications, 1999), 946.

Sacristy, he becomes the first person arriving in the Church each Sunday morning to get things ready for the Priest.

The prayer life of the Priest each day and especially before each Divine Liturgy is essential. "The Celebrant who lives in a hesychastic way before, during and after the Divine Liturgy, penetrates the depths of its spirit, which is the spirit of Christ's self-emptying."[136] "And being found in appearance as a man, He humbled Himself by becoming obedient to the point of death: death on a cross."[137] Jesus died on the Cross to save us from our sins. He bore our grief and sorrow to the fullest extent of His humanity. "For He made Him who knew no sin *to be* sin for us, that we might become the righteousness of God in Him."[138] Just as Jesus bore the sins of the world upon His shoulders, "the hesychast Priest, who has learnt through noetic prayer to accept the sin of others, the sin of all humanity, lives through the Holy Liturgy like a Martyr."[139] As the Priest's assistant during the Mass, the Deacon must seize the initiative and become the first to arrive each Sunday morning to prepare for Mass.

After these preliminary chores, the Deacon prepares the Sacred Vessels for use in the Divine Liturgy. The purificator is placed on top of and partially tucked inside the Chalice, with the paten, the host, and the pall laid right above. The prepared Chalice is vested with a veil bearing the liturgical color of the day. The burse containing the corporal are placed upon the credence table. The Ciborium with hosts is

---

[136] Metropolitan of Nafpaktos Hierotheos, *Hesychia and Theology: The Context for Man's Healing in the Orthodox Church*, 446.

[137] Philippians 2:8 NASB.

[138] 2 Corinthians 5:21 NKJV.

[139] Metropolitan of Nafpaktos Hierotheos, *Hesychia and Theology: The Context for Man's Healing in the Orthodox Church*, 446.

prepared and sits to the right of the veiled Chalice upon the credence table.

The Deacon's final preparation for Mass involves setting the ribbon in the Holy Gospel Book and practicing his chant. During the Mass, this is the Deacon's most important liturgical assignment: Proclaiming the Gospel of Jesus Christ. "St. Jerome († 420) speaks of the deacon as reader of the Gospel."[140] During our Divine Liturgy, after the Epistle is chanted by the Subdeacon, the Deacon places the Gospel book at the center of the Holy Altar. "The sacred Altar is the focal point of the worshipping congregation, because there the Sacrament of the divine Eucharist is celebrated. The fact that the Book of the Gospels lies upon it demonstrates the connection between Holy Scripture and worship."[141] Singing the Gospel is a Deacon's greatest joy. "From the Vth century, this became more and more the deacon's special privilege. It was natural that the highest assistant at Mass should perform the highest office, after that of actually consecrating."[142]

After the incense is charged, the Deacon kneels on the footpace and prays, "Cleanse my heart and my lips, O almighty God, who didst cleanse the lips of the prophet Isaiah with a burning coal; vouchsafe through Thy gracious mercy so to cleanse me that I may worthily proclaim Thy holy Gospel. Through Christ our Lord. Amen."[143] During our High Solemn Mass each Sunday and most feast days, the Thurifer leads the way with the candle-bearing Acolytes, the Mas-

---

[140] Adrian Fortescue, *The Mass: A Study of the Roman Liturgy*, 280.

[141] Metropolitan of Nafpaktos Hierotheos, *Hesychia and Theology: The Context for Man's Healing in the Orthodox Church*, 181.

[142] Adrian Fortescue, *The Mass: A Study of the Roman Liturgy*, 280-281.

[143] Dom Gaspar Lefebvre, *The Saint Andrew Daily Missal*, 960.

ter of Ceremonies, the Subdeacon, and the Deacon holding the golden Gospel book high, all processing in place for the chanted proclamation in the nave.

Another diaconate duty occurs during the Canon of the Mass. Most every liturgical movement of the Priest is mirrored by the Deacon as the two seem united as one. During my Roman Catholic childhood, the structure of the Mass was changed significantly, the Priest facing the people in the pews rather than seeming to take the people's prayers directly towards heaven as he faced the Holy Altar. The prayers of the Canon of the Mass span the centuries and are eminently beautiful and powerfully profound. With the words of consecration, we are reminded:

> Verily, verily I say unto you,
> Except ye eat the flesh of the Son of man, and drink his blood,
> ye have no life in you.
> Whoso eateth my flesh, and drinketh my blood, hath eternal life;
> and I will raise him up at the last day.
> For my flesh is meat indeed, and my blood is drink indeed.
> He that eateth my flesh and drinketh my blood,
> dwelleth in me, and I in him.
> As the living Father has sent me, and I live by the Father:
> so he that eateth me, even he shall live by me.[144]

During our Western Rite Mass, the Deacon holds the chalice with the Blood of Christ for the Priest to tincture the Body

---

[144] Luke 6:53-57 NKJV.

of Christ, placing the Eucharist on the tongues of the faithful at the altar rail.

Just prior to the Priest's blessing at the end of the Divine Liturgy, the Deacon leads the congregation in singing the *Ita, missa est*, literally meaning, "Go, you have been dismissed." The Priest blesses the people, proclaims the Last Gospel John 1:1-14, and leads the congregation with a closing prayer to Our Lady. After genuflecting before the Holy Altar, the ministers and servers process from the sanctuary through the nave during the recessional hymn before returning to the Sacristy for our final prayers.

During a typical Sunday morning, we begin Lauds at 9:00 a.m. with our Divine Liturgy and finish our morning worship nearly two-and-a-half hours later. Yet regardless of whether I serve at the Holy Altar or sit in choir with the Acolytes during Mass, this time of worship has been and remains timeless. It seems like a mere fifteen or twenty minutes. Although innumerable liturgical words many centuries old are spoken and sung during these hours of worship, a profound peace, exemplified by poignant pauses in the midst of the sung psalms of Lauds, permeates our communal prayer. This deep and abiding experience of the power and presence of God is the source of infinite joy and abundant grace. When immersed in still silence, our liturgical experience of God is much magnified.

CHAPTER SEVEN

JOYFUL SOLITUDE

Now as He was going out on the road, one came running, knelt before Him, and asked Him, "Good Teacher, what shall I do that I may inherit eternal life?" So Jesus said to him, "Why do you call Me good? No one *is* good but One, *that is*, God. You know the commandments: 'Do not commit adultery,' 'Do not murder,' 'Do not steal,' 'Do not bear false witness,' 'Do not defraud,' 'Honor your father and your mother.' " And he answered and said to Him, "Teacher, all these things I have kept from my youth." Then Jesus, looking at him, loved him, and said to him, "One thing you lack: Go your way, sell whatever you have and give to the poor, and you will have treasure in heaven; and come, take up the cross, and follow Me." But he was sad at this word, and went away sorrowful, for he had great possessions. Then Jesus looked around and said to His disciples, "How hard it is for those who have riches to enter the kingdom of God!" And the disciples were astonished at His words. But Jesus answered again and said to them, "Children, how hard it is for those who trust in riches to enter the kingdom of God! It is easier for a camel to go through the eye of a needle than for a rich man to enter the kingdom of God." And they were greatly astonished, saying among themselves, "Who then can be saved?" But Jesus looked at them and said, "With men *it is* impossible, but not with God; for with God all things are possible." Then Peter began to say to Him, "See, we have left all and followed you." So Jesus answered and said, "Assuredly, I say to you, there is no one who has left house or brothers or sisters or father or mother or wife or children or lands, for My sake and the gospel's, who shall not receive a hundredfold now in this time–houses and brothers and sisters and mothers and children and lands, with persecutions–and in the age to come, eternal life. But many *who are* first will be last, and the last first" (Mark 10:17-31 NKJV).

"Is it possible to pass from loneliness to solitude?"[145] We face varying degrees of loneliness in our lives, and nearly all of us experienced a deeper and more intense loneliness during the recent global pandemic. The sacramental life of the Holy Orthodox Church is the best cure for loneliness.

Pascha is the central feast of our Orthodox faith. Both at Christmas and Pascha, our church welcomes many into the full experience of our church through the Sacraments of Baptism, Chrismation, and Holy Communion. "In the early Church the celebration of baptism took place during the solemn Easter vigil, and in fact, the Easter liturgy grew out of the 'Paschal mystery' of baptism."[146] As a Deacon, I find tears in my eyes during many Baptisms of both young and old alike. "Holy Church teaches us that every Christian receives from God at holy baptism a holy guardian angel who

---

[145] Sister Vivian Whitehead, 12 October 1978, Theology and Community Service, University of Notre Dame, Notre Dame, IN, Journal Comment.

[146] Alexander Schmemann, *For the Life of the World*, 68.

invisibly guards the Christian, guides him to every good work throughout the whole course of his life, and reminds him of the commandments of God. So, too, there is a prince of darkness who wants to drag the whole human race to its ruin and who assigns to each person one of the evil spirits who follows the person everywhere and tries to draw him into every form of sin."[147]

Orthodox people sin. The Sacrament of Confession offers forgiveness and healing. Sin strikes at the heart of every believer, from the monks and nuns in monastic life to both single and married people in the pews of our churches. "Against some monks of extremely attentive and recollected life who have preserved bodily virginity, the spirit of impurity hurls himself with special fury."[148] Yet each of us have our own particular sins and vices to battle and with God's grace overcome. Baptism is the beginning. Confession helps us along the way. The Eucharist further purifies our souls and strengthens our resolve. "As He washes them in Baptism He cleanses them from the filth of wickedness and imposes His own form upon them; when He anoints them He activates the energies of the Spirit of which He, for the sake of our flesh, became the Treasury. But when He has led the initiate to the table and has given him His body to eat He entirely changes him, and transforms him into His own state."[149]

Baptism, Chrismation, and the Eucharist are inexorably linked because "baptism and chrismation were always fulfilled in the Eucharist–which is the sacrament of the Church's

[147] Bishop Ignatius Brianchaninov, *The Arena: Guidelines for Spiritual and Monastic Life*, 163.

[148] Ibid., 178.

[149] Nicholas Cabasilas, *The Life in Christ* (Crestwood, NY: St. Vladimir's Seminary Press, 1974), 113.

ascension to the Kingdom, the sacrament of the 'world to come.' "[150] The highlight of my week each and every week remains constant: Receiving the Body and Blood of Christ during the Divine Liturgy. "He who eats My flesh and drinks My blood abides in Me, and I in him."[151] The reception of the Body and Blood of Christ, the Corpus Christi and Precious Blood, merges the infinity of heaven with our finite earthly existence. This precise moment during the Divine Liturgy is when we experience our uncreated God most directly. Upon receiving the Eucharist, we receive the Holy Trinity, because God as Father, Son, and Spirit is undivided.

"The Good that is beyond being and beyond the unoriginate is one, the holy unity of three persons, Father, Son and Holy Spirit. It is an infinite union of three infinites."[152] Three infinite persons, one infinite God. "There is one God, because the Father is the begetter of the unique Son and the fount of the Holy Spirit: one without confusion and three without division. The Father is unoriginate Intellect, the unique essential Begetter of the unique Logos, also unoriginate, and the fount of the unique everlasting life, the Holy Spirit."[153]

We experience joyful solitude to the extent we fully participate in the Divine Liturgy. "The Divine Liturgy is an indescribably magnificent feast."[154] Within our Orthodox

---

[150] Alexander Schmemann, *For the Life of the World*, 68.

[151] John 6:56 NKJV.

[152] Saint Maximos the Confessor, "Various Texts on Theology, the Divine Economy, and Virtue and Vice," *The Philokalia*, vol. 2, compiled by Saint Nikodemos and Saint Makarios, translated and edited by G.E.H. Palmer, Philip Sherrard, and Kallistos Ware (New York: Faber and Faber, 1981), 164.

[153] Ibid., 165.

[154] Deacon David Lochbihler, *The Joy of Orthodoxy*, 20.

tradition, "Feast means *joy.*"[155] Besides experiencing an almost timeless joy at Mass, we pray in solitude and ponder the great mysteries of our faith. The Trinity and receiving the Body and Blood of Christ are two of our Orthodox Faith's most profound mysteries. "The Trinity is, for the Orthodox Church, the unshakable foundation of all religious thought, of all piety, of all spiritual life, of all experience. It is the Trinity that we pursue in seeking after God, when we search for the fullness of being, for the end and meaning of existence."[156] We commune in joyful solitude with the undivided Holy Trinity every time we receive Holy Communion. "There is one God because there is one Divinity, a Unity unoriginate, simple, beyond being, without parts and undivided."[157]

Another superb source of joyful solitude in our lives involves the nurturing of a deep and abiding love for Our Lady, the Theotokos, the Blessed Virgin Mary. Mary is the Mother of God. Mary is Jesus' mom. Contemplating these two truths in silence and solitude lead to a deep and abiding joy in one's heart. "For just as He Himself became man without changing His nature or altering His power, so He who makes her who bore Him a Mother while keeping her a Virgin."[158] The Theotokos is doubly honoured as both the Blessed Virgin Mary and the Holy Mother of God.

Focusing one's heart upon the miraculous Nativity and Childhood of Jesus offers innumerable opportunities to pray with joyful solitude. Prayerfully contemplating a dear mother

---

[155] Alexander Schmemann, *For the Life of the World*, 63 (emphasis in original).

[156] Vladimir Lossky, *The Mystical Theology of the Eastern Church*, 65.

[157] Saint Maximos the Confessor, "Various Texts on Theology, the Divine Economy, and Virtue and Vice," *The Philokalia*, vol. 2, 165.

[158] Ibid., 166.

and her beloved offspring leads to an array of additional questions, two coming most readily to mind: "How did a mother after giving birth remain a virgin? How was He who was supremely perfect develop as He grew up (cf. Luke 2 : 52)?"[159]

The first mystery before us is that of the Virgin Mother. The Virgin Mary asked a similar question of the Archangel Gabriel. "Then said Mary unto the angel, How shall this be, seeing I know not a man?"[160] Gabriel's response, a source of immense joy for humanity, may be pondered in silence and solitude for an eternity without being fully understood. "And the angel answered and said unto her, The Holy Ghost shall come upon thee, and the power of the Highest shall overshadow thee: therefore also that holy thing which shall be born shall be called the Son of God."[161]

The second mystery before us involves Jesus the Messiah, the Son of God:

> Let the same mind be in you that was in Christ Jesus,
> who, though he existed in the form of God
> > did not regard equality with God
> > as something to be grasped,
> but emptied himself
> > taking the form of a slave,
> > assuming human likeness.
> And being found in appearance as a human,
> > he humbled himself
> > and became obedient to the point of death–

---

[159] Ibid., 167-168.
[160] Luke 1:34 KJV.
[161] Luke 1:35 KJV.

even death on a cross.[162]

Jesus "in the form of God" took "the form of a bondservant" and came "in appearance as a man."[163] The New Testament Greek teaches us that although Jesus' *schema* was that of a man, His *morphe* included His identity as both God and bondservant. In other words, Jesus' *schema*, what men saw on the outside, revealed only a man, but his *morphe*, who He was deep down inside, included His identity as both God and bondservant.

"If it is understood that Christ's 'co-nature' with us is Christianity's greatest joy and depth, that he is a genuine human being and not some phantom or bodiless apparition, that He is one of us and forever united to us through His humanity, then devotion to Mary also becomes understandable, for she is the one who gave Him His human nature, His flesh and blood."[164] This mysterious reality allows us to begin an adventure for all eternity, loving the God-Man Jesus born from the womb of the Virgin-Mother Mary.

"Despite our sins and mortality, it remains our created end to become gods, beginning in this life."[165] The Blessed Virgin Mary freely assented to the angelic invitation from the Almighty to become the Mother of God: "Behold the handmaid of the Lord; be it unto me according to thy word."[166]

---

[162] Philippians 2:5-8 NRSV.

[163] Philippians 2:6-8 NKJV.

[164] Alexander Schmemann, "The Virgin Mary," *Celebration of Faith*, vol. 3, translated by John A. Jillions (Crestwood, NY: St. Vladimir's Seminary Press, 1995), 23.

[165] Christopher A. Beeley, *Gregory of Nazianzus on the Trinity and the Knowledge of God* (New York: Oxford University Press, 2008), 118.

[166] Luke 1:38a KJV.

An indescribable and inexplicable divine mystery occurred within the womb of the Theotokos: "In the womb of Mary, God and man were joined."[167]

"And, to put the most important last, how did God become man? And – what is even more mysterious – how did the Logos, while subsisting wholly, essentially and hypostatically in the Father, also exist essentially and hypostatically in the flesh? How is He who is wholly God by nature become wholly man by nature, not renouncing either nature in any way at all, neither the divine, through which He is God, nor ours, through which He became man? Faith alone can embrace these mysteries, for it is faith that makes real for us things beyond intellect and reason (cf. Heb. 11 : 1)."[168] The joy of our Orthodox journey finds its source in the inexplicable link between the Logos and the Theotokos. "In patristic Logos doctrine the incommunicable gulf between the absolute simplicity of the transcendent God, and the diffused world of immanent reality (the distance between the unchanging One and the variable Many), had been bridged by the divine Logos."[169]

Our next challenge is to focus in prayer and solitude upon these divine mysteries. This contemplation inevitably leads to love. "It is not simply to 'know' about him and his doctrine, but to *know him*–living and abiding among those who love him."[170]

....

[167] Saint John Maximovitch, *The Orthodox Veneration of the Mother of God*, 25.

[168] Saint Maximos the Confessor, "Various Texts on Theology, the Divine Economy, and Virtue and Vice," *The Philokalia*, vol. 2, 168.

[169] John McGuckin, *Saint Cyril of Alexandria and the Christological Controversy*, 177.

[170] Alexander Schmemann, *The Eucharist* (Crestwood, NY: St.

....
Vladimir's Seminary Press, 1987), 128-129.

EPILOGUE

STILL SILENCE DURING THE DIVINE LITURGY

"For My flesh is food indeed, and my blood is drink indeed. He who eats My flesh and drinks My blood abides in Me, and I in him (John 6:55-56 NKJV).

"Blessed *are* the pure in heart: for they shall see God."[171] This is where we begin. "In the language of the monastic fathers, all prayer, reading, meditation and all the activities of the monastic life are aimed at *purity of heart*, an unconditional and totally humble surrender to God, a total acceptance of ourselves and of our situation as willed by him."[172]

Truly the Divine Liturgy contains "our whole theology," and our participation in the Divine Liturgy nurtures God's call for us to "become divine partakers."[173] Each Divine Liturgy, we are immersed in a reality and depth both indescribable and beyond our comprehension. "God *is* a Spirit: and they that worship him must worship *him* in spirit and

---

[171] Matthew 5:8 KJV.

[172] Thomas Merton, *Contemplative Prayer*, 68.

[173] His Eminence Metropolitan Joseph, Antiochian House of Studies, 4 September 2015, Antiochian Village Conference Center, Bolivar, PA, Divine Liturgy.

in truth."[174] Touching the "heavenly places"[175] here on earth, we are blessed to become "partakers of the divine nature."[176]

"The divine liturgy–the continual ascent, the lifting up of the Church to *heaven*, to the throne of glory, to the unfading light and joy of the kingdom of God–is the focus of this experience, simultaneously its source and presence, gift and fulfillment. 'Standing in the temple of thy glory we think we are in heaven.' These words are not pious rhetoric, for they express the very essence, the very purpose both of the Church and of her worship as above all precisely a *liturgy*, an action (ἔργον), in which the essence of what is taking place is simultaneously revealed and fulfilled."[177]

The greatest joy of my life is being called to serve as a Deacon during the Divine Liturgy at Saint Patrick Orthodox Church. Our Western Rite Mass of Saint Gregory the Great is historically a very ancient Orthodox liturgical service. It is such a humbling experience to be so close to God at the Holy Altar during the Mass. "We unite ourselves to Him, in so far as this is possible, by participating in the godlike virtues and by entering into communion with Him through prayer and praise. Because the virtues are similitudes of God, to participate in them puts us in a fit state to receive the Deity, yet it does not actually unite us to Him. But prayer through its sacral and hieratic power actualizes our ascent to and union with the Deity, for it is a bond between noetic creatures and their Creator."[178] The finite

---

[174] John 4:24 KJV.

[175] Ephesians 1:3 NRSV.

[176] 2 Peter 1:4b NKJV.

[177] Alexander Schmemann, *The Eucharist*, 165.

[178] Saint Gregory Palamas, "Three Texts on Prayer and Purity of Heart," *The Philokalia*, vol. 4, compiled by Saint Nikodemos and Saint

strives for the infinite; although as created beings we never reach our goal, this yearning for the uncreated is both timeless and profound.

"And Jesus called a little child unto him, and set him in the midst of them, And said, Verily I say unto you, Except ye be converted, and become as little children, ye shall not enter into the kingdom of heaven. Whosoever therefore shall humble himself as this little child, the same is greatest in the kingdom of heaven. And whoso shall receive one such little child in my name receiveth me."[179] Besides approaching the Holy Altar of the Almighty in humility, much joy accrues in our hearts to the extent we stand in joyful anticipation of the miraculous occurrence each and every Mass. "We must be children and poets if we would experience Christ incarnate in our lives, because we must touch the immediacy of life again, as at creation itself."[180] Truly we witness a miracle with the child's eyes of faith each Sunday upon seeing the bread and wine transformed into the Body and Blood of Christ.

"Christian faith begins with the encounter with Christ, with the reception of him as the Son of God, who manifests the Father and his love to us."[181] This intimate encounter is immediately experienced upon receiving the very same Body and Blood of Christ minutes later in the Divine Liturgy during Holy Communion. Too often in our lives, even during the holiest of feasts, we fail to perceive what is happening with a child's innocent awareness. "If we have lost

---

Makarios, translated and edited by G.E.H. Palmer, Philip Sherrard, and Kallistos Ware (New York: Faber and Faber, 1995), 343.

[179] Matthew 18:2-5 KJV.

[180] Metropolitan Philip Saliba and Joseph J. Allen, *Meeting the Incarnate God*, 48.

[181] Alexander Schmemann, *The Eucharist*, 167.

touch, it is because we have come to value efficiency rather than tenderness, to manage life rather than to feel it, to surrender devotion rather than to develop it."[182]

A rich prayer life and a love for the Word of God helps us remember the deep Eucharistic theology of the Gospel of John. "Then Jesus said unto them, Verily, verily, I say unto you, Except ye eat the flesh of the Son of man, and drink his blood, ye have no life in you. Whoso eateth my flesh, and drinketh my blood, hath eternal life; and I will raise him up at the last day. For my flesh is meat indeed, and my blood is drink indeed."[183] What exactly happens upon receiving the Eucharist? "So we dwell in Him and are indwelt and become one spirit with Him. The soul and the body and all their faculties forthwith become spiritual, for our souls, our bodies and blood, are united with His."[184] Put more simply, "Christ infuses Himself into us and mingles Himself with us."[185] Ponder the utterly unimaginable: Jesus lives is us, and we live in Jesus. "He dwells in us, and He is our dwelling place."[186]

From there we return to our union and communion with the Holy Trinity. "Being offered in the Son, it is offered to the Father. Being offered to the Father, it is fulfilled in the partaking of the Holy Spirit. And therefore the eucharist is the eternally living and lifecreating source of the Church's knowledge of the Most Holy Trinity."[187] God the Father, God the Son, and God the Holy Ghost are never divided, never

---

[182] Metropolitan Philip Saliba and Joseph J. Allen, *Meeting the Incarnate God*, 48.

[183] John 6:53-55 KJV.

[184] Nicholas Cabasilas, *The Life in Christ*, 116.

[185] Ibid., 123.

[186] Ibid., 115.

[187] Alexander Schmemann, *The Eucharist*, 167.

apart. "This acceptance of the Son, this union in him with the Father, is fulfilled as salvation, as the new life, as the kingdom of God in the communion of the Holy Spirit, which is the divine life itself, communion with God. And thus, the eucharist is also the sacrament of our *access* to God and knowledge of him and union with him."[188]

We immerse ourselves in the still silence of the Divine Liturgy and become united to our Almighty Creator in an indescribable way beyond human comprehension. "As we partake of His human Body and Blood we receive God Himself into our souls. It is thus God's Body and Blood which we receive, His soul, mind, and will, no less than those of His humanity."[189] Our humanity touches God's divinity. "A man is returned to that place that God had prepared for him when he created the world. He stands at the heights, before the throne of God; he stands in heaven, before the face of God himself, and freely, in the fulness of love and knowledge, uniting in himself the whole world, all creation, he offers thanksgiving, and in him the whole world affirms and acknowledges this thanksgiving to be 'meet and right.' This man is Christ. He alone is without sin, he alone is Man in all the fulness of his purpose, calling and glory."[190]

The Holy Eucharist within the Divine Liturgy in still silence leads us to heaven itself. "It is all a sacrament and experience of his presence: of the Son of God, who came down from heaven and was incarnate that he might in himself lead us up to heaven."[191] Because of this intimate interaction, we truly may

---

[188] Ibid.
[189] Nicholas Cabasilas, *The Life in Christ*, 122.
[190] Alexander Schmemann, *The Eucharist*, 170.
[191] Ibid., 199.

be saved. "Salvation is complete. After the darkness of sin, the fall and death, a man once again offers to God the pure, sinless, free and perfect thanksgiving."[192] Eucharist is thanksgiving.

As we experience heaven on earth during the Divine Liturgy, we walk ever so slowly, in His grace and will, towards our eternal home in heaven. "Growth towards God *never ends*. In the whole of our human life we are called into 'God-likeness'; we are to become like God, to struggle toward the ultimate objective of all human endeavor in θέωσις [*theosis*: 'deification' or 'divinization']."[193] We as created strive to be one with the Uncreated. "The one born of God, knowing him, gives thanks, and in giving thanks he is free, and the power and miracle of thanksgiving, as freedom and liberation, lies in the fact that it *makes the unequal equal*: God and man, creature and Creator, servant and Master."[194]

This movement is beyond human understanding "Deification is in fact beyond every name."[195] Yet deification begins and reaches fruition in the celebration of the Holy Eucharist with the person and presence of Jesus Christ. "He alone in himself restores the 'fallen image' and raises it to God, and thus we now offer the thanksgiving of Christ, hear it and take part in it, when the celebrant begins the eucharistic prayer commanded to us by Christ, who has united us for all ages with God."[196]

---

[192] Ibid., 170.

[193] Joseph J. Allen, *Inner Way: Toward a Rebirth of Eastern Christian Spiritual Direction* (Brookline, MA: St. Vladimir's Seminary Press, 2000), 43 (emphasis in original).

[194] Alexander Schmemann, *The Eucharist*, 180 (emphasis in original).

[195] Gregory Palamas, *The Triads*, edited by John Meyendorff and translated by Nicholas Gendle (Mahwah, NJ: Paulist Press, 1983), 87.

[196] Alexander Schmemann, *The Eucharist*, 170.

Our best friends in life, both now and into eternity, are Jesus and Mary. Although deification may be experienced yet not properly named, our best friends Jesus and Mary lead us there. We receive the Body and Blood of Jesus Christ during the Divine Liturgy. The Blessed Virgin Mary "is the one through whom Christ can always call Himself 'The Son of Man.' Son of God, Son of Man… God descending and becoming man so that man could become divine, could become a partaker of the divine nature (2 Pet. 1:4), or as the teachers of the Church expressed it, 'deified.' Precisely here, in this extraordinary revelation of man's authentic nature and calling, is the source of that gratitude and tenderness which cherishes Mary as our link to Christ and, in Him, to God. And nowhere is this reflected more clearly than in the Nativity of the Mother of God."[197]

And so we return to the beginning. I rejoice to celebrate each year the Feast of the Nativity of the Blessed Virgin Mary on 8 September when nearly a decade ago at Saint Patrick Orthodox Church I finally came home, anointed and consecrated with the Chrism Oil, forever welcomed into the bosom of our beloved Holy Orthodox Church. I was baptized at Saint Patrick Catholic Church in Chesterton, Indiana, very soon after birth more than sixty-five years ago. Little did I know I would receive the Holy Chrism as an Orthodox convert fifty-six years later at Saint Patrick Orthodox Church in Bealeton, Virginia. "He is your glory and He is your God, who has done these great and awesome things for you which your eyes have seen."[198]

---

[197] Alexander Schmemann, "The Virgin Mary," *Celebration of Faith*, vol. 3, 23.

[198] Deuteronomy 10:21 NASB.

BIBLIOGRAPHY

Allen, Joseph J., ed. *And He Leads Them*. Ben Lomond, CA: Conciliar Press, 2001.

_____. *Inner Way: Toward a Rebirth of Eastern Christian Spiritual Direction*. Brookline, MA: St. Vladimir's Seminary Press, 2000.

Athanasius. *The Life of Antony and the Letter to Marcellinus*. Translated by Robert C. Gregg. Mahwah, NJ: Paulist Press, 1980.

_____. Saint. *On the Incarnation*. Crestwood, NY: St. Vladimir's Seminary Press, 1996.

Beeley, Christopher B. *Gregory of Nazianzus on the Trinity and the Knowledge of God*. New York: Oxford University Press, 2008.

Bennett, Rod. *Four Witnesses: The Early Church in Her Own Words*. San Francisco: Ignatius Press, 2002.

Blake, William. "Auguries of Innocence." *The Poetical Works of William Blake*. Edited by John Sampson. London: Oxford University, 1934.

Brianchaninov, Bishop Ignatius. *The Arena: Guidelines for Spiritual and Monastic Life.* Jordanville, NY: Holy Trinity Publications, 2012.

Cabasilas, Nicholas. *The Life in Christ.* Crestwood, NY: St. Vladimir's Seminary Press, 1974.

Cassian, Saint John. "On the Eight Vices." *The Philokalia*, vol. 1. Compiled by Saint Nikodemos and Saint Makarios, translated and edited by G.E.H. Palmer, Philip Sherrard, and Kallistos Ware. New York: Faber and Faber, 1979.

Conairis, Anthony M. *God and You: Person to Person.* Minneapolis, MN: Light & Life Publishing, 2005.

Cyprian. *On the Lord's Prayer: Tertullian, Cyprian, Origen.* Translated by Alistair Stewart-Sykes. Crestwood, NY: St. Vladimir's Seminary Press, 2004.

Dragas, Protopresbyter George Dion. *On the Priesthood and the Holy Eucharist.* Rollinsford, NH: Orthodox Research Institute, 2004.

Evagrios the Solitary. "On Prayer: One Hundred and Fifty-Three Texts." *The Philokalia*, vol. 1. Compiled by Saint Nikodemos and Saint Makarios, translated and edited by G.E.H. Palmer, Philip Sherrard, and Kallistos Ware. New York: Faber and Faber, 1979.

Fortescue, Adrian. *The Mass: A Study of the Roman Liturgy*, 2nd ed. London: Longmans, Green and Co., 1937.

Frazier, Millie Ruth. Letter to David Lochbihler. 11 September 2022.

———. Letter to David Lochbihler. 13 September 2022.

Friedrich, Kai. Personal Communication. Saint Patrick Orthodox Church. Bealeton, VA. 19 June 2021.

Gebhardt, Subdeacon John Wiley. Personal Communication. Saint Patrick Orthodox Church. Bealeton, VA. 19 June 2021.

Germanus of Constantinople, Saint. *On the Divine Liturgy*. Translated by Paul Meyendorff. Crestwood, NY: St. Vladimir's Seminary Press, 1984.

Gregorios, Hieromonk. *The Divine Liturgy: A Commentary in the Light of the Fathers*. Mount Athos Koutloumousiou Monastery, Greece: Cell of St John the Theologian, 2009.

Hierotheos, Metropolitan of Nafpaktos. *Hesychia and Theology: The Context for Man's Healing in the Orthodox Church*. Translated by Sister Pelagia Selfe. Levadia, Greece: Birth of the Theotokos Monastery, 2007.

Hopkins, Gerard Manley. *Poems of Gerard Manley Hopkins*, 3rd ed. Edited by W. H. Gardner. New York & London: Oxford University Press, 1948.

Ignatius of Antioch, Saint. "The Letters of Ignatius of Antioch: Ephesians 19:1." Translated by Robert M. Grant. *The Order of St. Ignatius of Antioch*, 5th ed. Englewood, NJ: Order of St. Ignatius of Antioch, 2006.

John, His Grace Bishop. Western Rite Vicariate Conference. 9 August 2018. St. Peter Orthodox Church, Fort Worth, TX. Lecture.

Joseph, His Eminence Metropolitan. Antiochian House of Studies. 4 September 2015. Antiochian Village Conference Center, Bolivar, PA. Divine Liturgy.

Lefebvre, Dom Gaspar. *The Saint Andrew Daily Missal*. Great Falls, MT: St. Bonaventure Publications, 1999.

Lochbihler, David. (1978). Theology and Community Service. University of Notre Dame, Notre Dame, IN. Journal Entry.

Lochbihler, Deacon David (in press). *The Holy Family*. Unpublished manuscript.

_____. *The Joy of Orthodoxy*. Nederland: Orthodox Logos, 2022.

Lossky, Vladimir. *The Mystical Theology of the Eastern Church*. Crestwood, NY: St. Vladimir's Seminary Press, 1976.

Markides, Kyriacos C. *The Mountain of Silence*. New York: Doubleday, 2001.

Mathewes-Green, Frederica. *The Lost Gospel of Mary: The Mother of Jesus in Three Ancient Texts*. Brewster, MA: Paraclete Press, 2007.

Maximos the Confessor, Saint. "Various Texts on Theology, the Divine Economy, and Virtue and Vice." *The Philokalia*, vol. 2. Compiled by Saint Nikodemos and Saint Makarios, translated and edited by G.E.H. Palmer, Philip Sherrard, and Kallistos Ware. New York: Faber and Faber, 1981.

Maximovitch, Saint John. *The Orthodox Veneration of the Mother of God*. Translated by Father Seraphim Rose. Platina, CA: St. Herman of Alaska Brotherhood, 2012.

McGuckin, John. *Saint Cyril of Alexandria and the Christological Controversy*. Crestwood, NY: St. Vladimir's Seminary Press, 1995.

Merton, Thomas. *Contemplative Prayer*. Garden City, NY: Image Books, 1971.

The Monastic Diurnal. London: Oxford University Press, 1963.

Nouwen, Henri J. M., Donald P. McNeill, and Douglas A. Morrison. *Compassion*. New York: Doubleday, 1982.

Palamas, Saint Gregory. *Mary the Mother of God: Sermons by Saint Gregory Palamas*. Edited by Christopher Veniamin. South Canaan, PA: Mount Thabor Publishing, 2005.

———. "Three Texts on Prayer and Purity of Heart." *The Philokalia*, vol. 4. Compiled by Saint Nikodemos and Saint Makarios, translated and edited by G.E.H. Palmer, Philip Sherrard, and Kallistos Ware. New York: Faber and Faber, 1995.

———. *The Triads*. Edited by John Meyendorff and translated by Nicholas Gendle. Mahwah, NJ: Paulist Press, 1983.

Peter of Damaskos. "Twenty-Four Discourses." *The Philokalia*, vol. 3. Compiled by Saint Nikodemos and Saint Makarios and translated and edited by G.E.H. Palmer, Philip Sherrard, and Kallistos Ware. New York: Faber and Faber, 1984.

The New Testament in Four Versions: King James, Revised Standard, Phillips Modern English, New English Bible. Washington, DC: Christianity Today, 1963.

"The Prayers to be Said While Vesting." Saint Patrick Orthodox Church Sacristy, Bealeton, VA, from Dom Gaspar Lefebvre. *The Saint Andrew Daily Missal*. Great Falls, MT: St. Bonaventure Publications, 1999.

The Orthodox Study Bible: New Testament and Psalms. Nashville, TN: Thomas Nelson Publishers, 1993.

Saint-Exupéry, Antoine de. *The Little Prince*. San Diego: Harcourt Brace, 1971.

Saliba, Metropolitan Philip and Joseph J. Allen, *Meeting the Incarnate God*. Brookline, MA: Holy Cross Orthodox Press, 2009.

Schmemann, Alexander. *The Eucharist*. Crestwood, NY: St. Vladimir's Seminary Press, 1987.

_____. *For the Life of the World*, 2nd ed. Crestwood, NY: St. Vladimir's Seminary Press, 1973.

_____. "The Virgin Mary." *Celebration of Faith*, vol. 3. Translated by John A. Jillions. Crestwood, NY: St. Vladimir's Seminary Press, 1995.

Sophrony, Archimandrite. *Saint Silouan the Athonite*. Translated by Rosemary Edmonds. Crestwood, NY: St. Vladimir's Seminary Press, 1991.

Symeon the New Theologian. *The Discourses*. Translated by C.J. deCatanzaro. Mahwah, NJ: Paulist Press, 1980.

Thomas, His Grace Bishop. Antiochian House of Studies. 2 September 2015. Antiochian Village Conference Center, Bolivar, PA. Lecture.

_____. Antiochian House of Studies, 3 September 2015. Antiochian Village Conference Center, Bolivar, PA. Graduation Banquet.

Tikhon of Voronezh, Saint. *From Things Earthly to Things Heavenly*. Translated by Marianna Lilley. Waynesboro, VA: Old Paths Press, 2020.

———. *On True Christianity*, vol. 1. Translated by Marianna Lilley. Waynesboro, VA: Old Paths Press, 2020.

Wordsworth, William. *Selected Poems of William Wordsworth.* Edited by Solomon Francis Gingerich. Boston: Houghton Mifflin Company, 1923.

Ware, Bishop Kallistos. *The Orthodox Way.* Crestwood, NY: St. Vladimir's Seminary Press, 1995.

Ware, Metropolitan Kallistos. "The Jesus Prayer in our Daily Lives." Saint Mark Coptic Orthodox Church, 23 June 2012, Fairfax, VA. Lecture.

Ware, Timothy. *The Orthodox Church.* London: Penguin Books, 1997.

Whitehead, Sister Vivian. (1978). Theology and Community Service. University of Notre Dame, Notre Dame, IN. Journal Comment.

ABOUT THE AUTHOR

Deacon David Lochbihler, J.D., celebrates ten years since his Chrismation at Saint Patrick Orthodox Church during the Feast of the Nativity of the Blessed Virgin Mary on Sunday 8 September 2013. He was ordained to the Holy Diaconate on Sunday 17 March 2019 during the Feast of Saint Patrick. Besides serving at Saint Patrick Orthodox Church, Deacon David teaches fourth grade at The Fairfax Christian School in Virginia. After graduating *summa cum laude* from the University of Notre Dame and *cum laude* from the University of Texas School of Law, Deacon David worked as a Chicago attorney for three years before becoming a teacher and coach for three decades. He earned Master's degrees in Elementary Education, Biblical Studies, and Orthodox Theology. His varsity high school basketball and soccer teams captured four N.V.I.A.C. conference championships. He authored *Prayers to Our Lady East and West* (2021), *The Joy of Orthodoxy* (2022), and *Our Orthodox Holy Family: A Joyful Journey with Jesus and Mary* (2023).

PRAYERS
TO OUR LADY
EAST AND WEST

DEACON DAVID LOCHBIHLER, J.D.

ORTHODOX LOGOS PUBLISHING

THE JOY OF ORTHODOXY

DEACON DAVID LOCHBIHLER, J.D.

ORTHODOX LOGOS PUBLISHING

DEACON DAVID LOCHBIHLER, J.D.

OUR ORTHODOX HOLY FAMILY:

A JOYFUL JOURNEY WITH JESUS AND MARY

ORTHODOX LOGOS PUBLISHING

Uitgeverij Orthodox Logos

- *De Orthodoxe Kerk: Verleden en heden* – Jean Meyendorff
- *Biecht en communie* – Alexander Schmemann
- *Verliefd Zijn op het Leven* – Samensteller: Maxim Hodak
- *De Orthodoxe Kerk* – Aartspriester Sergei Hackel
- *De mensenrechten in het licht van het Evangelie* – Nicolas Lossky
- *Geboren in Haat Herboren in Liefde* – Klaus Kenneth
- *Hegoumena Thaissia van Leouchino: brieven aan een novice*
- *Het Jezusgebed* – Een monnik van de oosterse kerk
- *Gebedenboek Voor Kinderen: Volgens De Orthodox Christelijke Traditie*
- *Dagboek Van Keizerin Alexandra* – Keizerin Alexandra
- *Mijn ontmoeting met Archimandriet Sophrony* – Aartspriester Silouan Osseel
- *Stap voor stap veranderen* – Vader Meletios Webber
- *De Weg Naar Binnen* – Metropoliet Anthony (Bloom) Van Sourozh
- *Geraakt door God's liefde* – Klooster van de Levenschenkende Bron Chania
- *De Heilige Silouan de Athoniet* – Archimandrite Sophrony
- *The Beatitudes: A Pathway to Theosis* – Christopher J. Mertens
- *De Kracht van de Naam* – Metropoliet Kallistos van Diokleia
- *De Orthodoxe Weg* – Metropoliet Kallistos van Diokleia
- *Serafim Van Sarov* – Irina Goraïnoff
- *Feesten van de Orthodoxe Kerk – een Leerzaam Kleurboek*
- *Catechetisch woord Over Het gebed van het Hart* – Aartspreiester Silouan Osseel
- *Naar de Eenheid?* – Leonide Ouspensky
- *Bidden Met Ikonen* – Jim Forest

- *Onze Gedachten Bepalen Ons Leven* – Vader Thaddeus Van Vitovnica
- *Alledaagse Heiligen En Andere Verhalen* – Archimandriet Tichon (Sjevkoenov)
- *Geestelijke Brieven* – Vader Jozef De Hesychast
- *Nihilisme* – Vader Serafim Rose
- *Gods Openbaring Aan Het Menselijk Hart* – Vader Serafim Rose
- *In De Kaukazus* – Monnik Merkurius
- *Terugkeer* – Archimandriet Nektarios Antonopoulos
- *Weest ook gij uitgebreid* – Archimandriet Zacharias (Zacharou)
- *De Orthodoxe Kerk* – Verleden en heden

- *Fruit of the Spirit: An Orthodox Anthology* – Deacon David Lochbihler, J.D.
- *Joyful Solitude* – Deacon David Lochbihler, J.D.
- *Our Orthodox Holy Family* – Deacon David Lochbihler, J.D.
- *Prayers to Our Lady East and West* – Deacon David Lochbihler, J.D.
- *The Joy of Orthodoxy* – Deacon David Lochbihler, J.D.
- *The Inner Cohesion between the Bible and the Fathers in Byzantine Tradition* – S.M. Roye
- *St. Germanus of Auxerre* – Howard Huws
- *Elder Anthimos Of Saint Anne's* – Dr. Charalambos M. Bousias
- *Orthodox Preaching as the Oral Icon of Christ* – James Kenneth Hamrick
- *The Final Kingdom* – Pyotr Volkov

ORTHODOX LOGOS PUBLISHING
www.orthodoxlogos.com

www.ingramcontent.com/pod-product-compliance
Lightning Source LLC
Chambersburg PA
CBHW031127080526
44587CB00011B/1143